SHAMELESS AUDACITY

How Black Women Can Find

Strength in the Teachings of Christ

NGOZI T. ROBINSON

I AM Publications

Shameless Audacity—How Black Women Can Find Strength in the Teachings of Christ

I AM Publications

(617) 564-1060

contact@iampubs.com

www.iampubs.com

ISBN: 978-1-943382-28-6

TABLE OF CONTENTS

Walking in Shameless Audacity

"Then Jesus said to them, "Suppose you have a friend, and you go to him at midnight and say, 'Friend, lend me three loaves of bread; a friend of mine on a journey has come to me, and I have no food to offer him.' And suppose the one inside answers, 'Don't bother me. The door is already locked, and my children and I are in bed. I can't get up and give you anything.' I tell you, even though he will not get up and give you the bread because of friendship, yet because of your shameless audacity he will surely get up and give you as much as you need."
—Luke 11:5-8 (NIV)

I am an African American woman and an ordained Baptist minister, and my life story has been shaped by both the witness of Scripture and the lived realities of Black womanhood in America. In a world that too often demands our silence or relegates our gifts to the background, I believe God invites us to embrace a spirit of shameless audacity. In the passage from Luke 11, Jesus tells a parable of a friend who knocks at midnight, refusing to be turned away. That persistent knocking—what some translations call "boldness," "importunity," or "shameless audacity"—is an image of how we are to approach God, life, and our calling. It is an attitude that refuses to quit, even when society says our dreams are too big or our voice is too loud.

Black women in particular have historically exhibited this type of unwavering faith, often drawing on our deep spiritual heritage to carry us through oppression, marginalization, and countless obstacles. Whether seeking healing from generational trauma or advocating for social justice, we tap into that God-given boldness—knocking on the door of opportunity, wisdom, and divine presence until we receive what we need. Yet despite our resilience, we still battle cultural forces that insist we play small, that we remain unnoticed, or that our strength is a liability rather than a gift.

In the pages of this book, I invite you to join me in rejecting that narrative. God has not called us to mere survival; God calls us to divine liberty—to think bigger, love deeper, and stand taller in the name of Christ. When we do, we embrace a shameless audacity that is both biblically grounded and profoundly liberating.

Shameless Audacity as an Invitation

We first encounter the idea of "shameless audacity" in Luke 11:5—10, where Jesus describes a scenario: someone goes to a friend at midnight, knocking persistently to request bread. Though the friend might not initially respond out of neighborly kindness, he eventually gives in to the man's request because of his persistence. The NRSV translates that key verse (Luke 11:8) with the word "persistence." Some older translations use "importunity," and others capture the spirit with terms like "boldness" or "shamelessness." No matter the wording, the overarching message is clear: God honors courageous faith that refuses to turn away empty-handed.

For Black women—whose stories are steeped in both pain and promise—this parable resonates on many levels. Our communities and households have long relied on strong, prayerful women who knock on heaven's door with unwavering conviction. Whether kneeling at an altar or marching in the streets, we carry the legacy of Harriet Tubman, Sojourner Truth, Ella Baker, and Fannie Lou Hamer—women who approached adversity head-on, clothed in the power of the Holy Spirit and guided by a burning commitment to justice.

That same "shameless audacity" is not mere stubbornness; it is faith in action, born of the knowledge that God can and will respond. We hold onto that hope not simply out of desperation but out of a real conviction that God is on the side of the oppressed. And so we press forward, believing that God's arms are open, God's resources are limitless, and God's love is unfailing.

The Call to Bold Persistence

To walk in shameless audacity means to come before God with confidence—pouring out our fears, pains, and aspirations without apology. It also means embracing our gifts, talents, and voices, refusing to let society dictate whether or how we should shine. When we accept this invitation, we align ourselves with God's radical intent to see all of creation flourish, especially those on the margins. We learn to stand firm in the face of systemic pressures that say "not now" or "not you," much like the friend in Jesus' parable who persists until the door is opened.

Why Focus on Black Women?

Across centuries, Black women have navigated overlapping layers of oppression—racism, sexism, classism—while managing family, community leadership, and personal faith journeys. Historically, we were encouraged to "stay in our place," whether on plantations, in segregated schoolrooms, or within male-dominated structures in society and church. Even today, cultural and institutional forces often push Black women to shrink themselves—whether that means diluting their natural leadership abilities or censoring their voices to maintain a fragile peace.

Yet, if we look to Scripture, there is no mandate for silence. On the contrary, the Bible overflows with accounts of women who stood their ground—Deborah, Ruth, Hannah, Mary Magdalene, and the Samaritan woman at the well, among others. Their stories challenge us to step fully into our God-given potential. For Black women in particular, the call to live boldly in Christ is a direct contradiction to messages of smallness we receive every day. Jesus reminds us that we are made in God's image and equipped to do greater works (cf. John 14:12).

The Collective Impact of Black Women's Success

In many Black churches, women are the backbone—filling the pews, leading committees, and anchoring ministries. Our success, spiritually and practically, translates into stronger families, flourishing congregations, and healthier communities. When Black women fully embrace their worth, talents, and calling, everyone benefits. Indeed, from the civil rights movement to modern-day activism, the strength and leadership of Black women have often shaped the moral conscience of entire nations.

By focusing on Black women, this book seeks to nurture that sacred boldness that already exists—too often hidden behind burdens of societal expectations. We will see how the teachings of Jesus offer us not only spiritual comfort but also a revolutionary blueprint for living large in faith, courage, and mission. In a world that frequently underestimates our potential, Jesus extends an invitation to "think big"—to push against any framework that constricts us and embrace God's boundless vision for our lives.

Liberation Theology and Womanist Theology

Before diving into the specific teachings of Jesus, it's helpful to understand the theological lenses that inform this book. Two powerful traditions—Liberation Theology and Womanist Theology—give us language and context for how the gospel speaks to social, political, and economic realities.

Liberation Theology

Liberation Theology grew out of Latin America in the late 1960s and 1970s, championed by theologians such as Gustavo Gutiérrez, Jon Sobrino, and Leonardo Boff. Its core premise is that God is on the side of the poor and oppressed, and that the gospel cannot be separated from concrete struggles for justice. Within this framework, salvation is not purely an individual, spiritual matter; it has real-world implications for dismantling oppressive systems and uplifting marginalized communities.

For Black women in the United States, the message of liberation resonates deeply. We see parallels in our own history—mass movements for civil rights, ongoing battles against systemic racism, and daily efforts to protect our families and neighborhoods from harm. Liberation Theology reminds us that God is not a distant observer but an active participant in our pursuit of freedom and dignity.

Womanist Theology

Womanist Theology, a term coined by writer Alice Walker and further developed by theologians like Katie Geneva Cannon, Jacquelyn Grant, and Delores Williams, centers the experiences, wisdom, and voices of Black women. It critiques mainstream theology for often neglecting or misinterpreting our lives and faith. Instead, Womanist Theology affirms that we encounter God most powerfully in our embodied realities—in our kitchens, workplaces, and pews—and that our everyday stories are crucial to understanding God's redemptive work in the world.

Rather than viewing theology as an academic exercise for a select few, womanist theologians invite us to see it as a living conversation about survival, resilience, and joy in the face of adversity. They insist that the unique struggles of Black women—ranging from colorism to economic exploitation—should not be relegated to the footnotes but placed at the center of how we do theology. In doing so, we discover that faith is not just about personal piety; it's about mutual uplift, communal wholeness, and a relentless quest for justice.

By drawing on both Liberation and Womanist Theology, this book offers a grounded, holistic perspective on why the teachings of Jesus speak so urgently to the realities of Black women today. We recognize that our faith is never divorced from our bodies or our social context. Instead, we embrace a Christ who heals, restores, and empowers us to press forward—fully embodied, fully heard, and fully free.

Structure and Purpose of the Book

This book is divided into ten chapters, each centered around a specific teaching of Jesus. From "Blessed Are the Poor in Spirit" (Matthew 5:3) to "I Have Come That They May Have Life . . . to the Full" (John 10:10), we will walk through key scriptural passages that illuminate the heart of Christ's message. These teachings are intentionally chosen for their relevance to Black women's lives—both the sorrows we bear and the hopes we carry.

Each chapter will include:
Biblical Context and Exegesis: We will explore the historical and cultural backdrop of each verse, considering how the original audience might have understood Jesus' words. This

section will help us grasp the depth and nuance of the Scripture, ensuring that we interpret it faithfully and apply it responsibly.

Womanist Reflection: Drawing on the legacy of Womanist Theology, we will examine how the passage speaks directly to Black women's experiences. We'll wrestle with questions like: What does this teaching mean for those who have been historically marginalized? Where does liberation and empowerment meet humble discipleship?

Practical Application: Lastly, we will consider real-world scenarios where these teachings come to life. Whether it's confronting micro-aggressions at work or nurturing our souls after seasons of burnout, we'll map out actionable steps. This could include spiritual disciplines, communal activities, advocacy work, or personal introspection—tangible ways to embody the message of Jesus.

Personal Reflection and Communal Growth
While each chapter provides theological insights and practical guidelines, this is not merely an intellectual exercise. My prayer is that you will engage each section with an open heart, using the journaling prompts or discussion questions to deepen your relationship with God and your community. Ultimately, discipleship is a shared journey. We draw strength from one another—our stories, our testimonies, our laughter, and even our tears.

Invitation to Transformation

Christianity is meant to be transformative. When Jesus declares in John 10:10, "I came that they may have life, and have it abundantly" (NRSV), He is not making a casual promise. He is offering us a new way of living, one in which we recognize our God-given worth and stretch beyond the limitations society imposes upon us. For Black women, this means shedding any shame, self-doubt, or resignation that keeps us from the fullness God intends.

Together, through the pages ahead, let us learn from Christ's words and let them shape our vision of who we are called to be. May we rediscover our capacity for shameless audacity, that tenacious faith which does not back down but presses in, trusting that God hears us—even at midnight—and will open doors that no one can shut.

A Final Word of Welcome

As we embark on this journey, let me offer a word of encouragement: You can show up big. You can rest in the truth that Jesus sees and values you. You can do the daring thing— whether that means launching a ministry, pursuing higher education, standing up against injustice, or finally giving yourself permission to rest. The biblical stories we explore and the theological reflections we share are all invitations to grow, heal, and testify to God's unfailing presence in our lives.

My prayer is that this book will challenge and comfort you in equal measure. Together, let us look to the teachings of Jesus not as distant relics of an ancient world but as living, breathing words that spark hope, courage, and liberation right here, right now.

Welcome to the journey of Shameless Audacity: How Black Women Can Find Strength in the Teachings of Christ. Let us walk forward boldly, hands joined, hearts expectant, and faith undaunted. Our midnight knock on heaven's door is not in vain—because God is ready to answer.

Chapter 1
"Blessed Are the Poor in Spirit" (Matthew 5:3)

"Blessed are the poor in spirit, for theirs is the kingdom of heaven."
—Matthew 5:3 (NRSV)

When we encounter the words of Jesus in the Gospel of Matthew—particularly in the Sermon on the Mount—we face a grand invitation to see our lives in light of God's kingdom. One of Jesus' most enduring and transformative teachings is found in the Beatitudes, a series of statements that challenge our assumptions about who is truly "blessed" and how. At first glance, "Blessed are the poor in spirit" might seem counterintuitive. We live in a society that prizes self-reliance, ambition, and the pursuit of personal gain. Yet Jesus calls us to a profound form of humility that resonates with a vision of community, justice, and reliance on God.

For Black women, these words carry a unique weight. Our experiences often sit at the intersection of multiple oppressions—racial, gender-based, economic—that test our resolve and emotional well-being. In such conditions, the notion of poverty of spirit can feel risky or even threatening; why would we choose vulnerability when the world can be so harsh? And yet, in the countercultural message of the Beatitudes lies a secret strength: the acknowledgement of our need for God does not diminish us—it empowers us, aligns us with divine resources, and knits us into the heart of a liberating gospel.

Contextualizing the Beatitudes

The Beatitudes appear at the beginning of the Sermon on the Mount (Matthew 5—7), a cornerstone of Jesus' teachings and one of the most quoted sections in all of Scripture. To appreciate the depth of these blessings, let's briefly explore their biblical setting and the radical implications they held for the first-century world—and how they continue to resonate today.

The Sermon on the Mount

Set on a hillside near the Sea of Galilee, the Sermon on the Mount was likely delivered to a diverse crowd of disciples and onlookers. Many were ordinary Galileans—fishermen, farmers, and tradespeople—living under Roman occupation. They had limited political or social power and often contended with heavy taxation. Into this environment, Jesus proclaimed a vision of a kingdom unlike any other—one where the poor, mourners, and peacemakers find themselves at the center of God's favor.

The sermon opens with the Beatitudes: a series of blessings that subvert the usual assumptions about status and success. Each blessing highlights a group that the broader culture might overlook or consider unlucky, yet Jesus assures them of divine favor. This promise extends not only to first-century believers but to every community that has found itself marginalized or overlooked, including African Americans in the United States.

A Countercultural Vision

The Sermon on the Mount is an invitation to live as citizens of God's reign. It turns worldly values upside down. Instead of extolling the powerful, the wealthy, or the outwardly successful, Jesus elevates those who are aware of their need for God, who hunger for righteousness, and who make peace. By beginning with "Blessed are the poor in spirit," He asserts that the greatest spiritual riches often emerge from a posture of humility and reliance on the divine.

This is countercultural in every age. Even now, we often measure success by career advancement, bank account balances, or social media followings. We may strive to appear confident and self-sufficient, fearing that to do otherwise is to fail. But the Beatitudes offer a radically different framework—one in which we find our true worth not in worldly accomplishments but in our alignment with God's priorities. This realignment is deeply relevant to Black women's lives, as we navigate systems that undervalue our contributions or reduce our identities to stereotypes. Jesus declares that those dismissed by the world are precisely the ones God calls blessed.

Poverty of Spirit and Liberation

"Blessed are the poor in spirit, for theirs is the kingdom of heaven."
—Matthew 5:3 (NRSV)

At the heart of this Beatitude lies a paradox: how can being "poor in spirit" lead to fullness in God's kingdom? Poverty of spirit is not about lacking self-esteem or cultivating a victim mentality. Rather, it involves an honest recognition of our dependence on God—of our spiritual neediness in a world that prefers self-reliance and pride. This humble posture has profound implications for justice, communal care, and our capacity to stand in solidarity with others who suffer.

Liberation Theology's Lens

Liberation theology affirms that God stands with the oppressed and marginalized. To be "poor in spirit" in this context means to stand open-handed before God, knowing that our help ultimately comes from the One who hears the cries of the brokenhearted (Psalm 34:18). This stance is deeply empowering for Black women who face structural injustices such as wage gaps, health disparities, or bias within church leadership. By acknowledging our vulnerability, we tap into divine power that counters oppression with holy resistance and transformative hope.

Poverty of spirit also propels us to empathize with others in need. When we recognize our own frailty, we become sensitive to the struggles of those around us. Theologian Gustavo Gutierrez famously wrote that "the preferential option for the poor" is central to understanding the gospel. For Black women, whose communities often battle poverty, displacement, and underfunded schools, poverty of spirit is not a passive state but a call to active solidarity. We find that God's kingdom belongs to those who refuse to pretend they are above needing help—and who likewise refuse to abandon those who cry out for liberation.

Vulnerability as Strength

In mainstream culture, vulnerability is frequently framed as a weakness. Yet "poor in spirit" reclaims vulnerability as an avenue to God's power. Scripture reminds us repeatedly that when we are weak, God's strength is made perfect within us (2 Corinthians 12:9). Rather than a cause for shame, vulnerability becomes a doorway to divine partnership.

For Black women who are often expected to embody the myth of the "strong Black woman," embracing vulnerability can be especially challenging. We may feel pressured to carry the weight of entire families and communities on our shoulders. We learn to suppress our own wounds and needs so that others feel less threatened, or so that we might protect ourselves from harmful stereotypes. However, living perpetually in hyper-independence exacts a steep toll on our mental and physical health. It can also isolate us from the communal nurturing we desperately need.

By contrast, embracing poverty of spirit releases us from that solitary burden. We realize we do not have to do it all alone. When we say to God, "I need You," we say it not in despair but in holy confidence that the Spirit stands ready to empower and uplift us. In fact, it is precisely in that moment of surrender that we align ourselves with God's expansive kingdom, where the last become first and the weary find rest.

Womanist Reflections

Womanist theology reminds us that Black women's faith is inseparable from our lived experiences. Our stories of survival, resilience, and creativity offer profound lessons about the spiritual posture of humility—and how it leads to freedom.

Historical Examples of "Poverty of Spirit"

Throughout history, Black women have embodied poverty of spirit in ways that fueled communal liberation. Consider Harriet Tubman, whose unwavering trust in God propelled her to lead hundreds of enslaved people to freedom. Despite the very real dangers of capture and death, Tubman's reliance on divine guidance became her wellspring of courage. Far from diminishing her abilities, her dependence on God sharpened her intuition and resilience.

Likewise, Sojourner Truth—born into slavery—relied on her deep spiritual convictions as she traveled the country advocating for abolition and women's rights. When she famously declared, "Ain't I a woman?" she not only questioned social structures but also pointed to the moral authority of a faith that embraces the oppressed. Her humility before God did not weaken her voice; rather, it empowered her to speak boldly to presidents, judges, and everyday citizens alike.

In both cases, these women's sense of limitation—financial, educational, or social—did not limit their impact. Their reliance on prayer, on divine wisdom, and on faith-filled action was the bedrock of their courage. That is the essence of poverty of spirit: knowing we do not have all the resources within ourselves but that we serve a God who does.

Communal Resilience

Historically, Black women have built powerful support systems—church mothers, prayer circles, mutual aid societies—that exemplify a womanist ethic of care. When any sister faced sickness, loss, or oppression, the community rallied with prayer, shared meals, and compassionate presence. This communal interdependence reflects poverty of spirit in action. Instead of claiming self-sufficiency, we collectively acknowledge our reliance on God and one another.

In contemporary contexts, womanist theologians such as Katie Geneva Cannon, Jacquelyn Grant, and Delores Williams emphasize that our faith practices must engage both body and spirit, lived reality and biblical revelation. Poverty of spirit thus becomes a collective stance as much as an individual one: we humble ourselves before God and each other, building solidarity that overthrows isolation. Through this stance, we reject any theology that demands docility in the face of injustice; rather, we find that genuine humility draws strength from God to stand against systems that crush human dignity.

Practical Steps: Embracing Spiritual Humility

Poverty of spirit need not remain an abstract concept. We can cultivate it through daily practices that nurture both our relationship with God and our connection to others. Below are some ways to integrate this Beatitude into your life, especially as a Black woman navigating a complex world.

Spiritual Disciplines

Prayer Journaling: Set aside time each day or week to write out your prayers, fears, and hopes. Be honest about where you feel inadequate or overwhelmed. Reflect on moments when you sensed God's presence guiding or comforting you. By documenting your spiritual journey, you create a tangible record of your dependence on God's grace.

Corporate Worship: Regular participation in congregational life—whether in a traditional church setting or a small group—helps anchor us in a community of faith. Singing hymns, listening to the Word preached, and participating in communal prayer remind us that we do not journey alone. We lean into the shared "poverty" that leads to God's abundant mercy.

Fasting and Almsgiving: Traditional disciplines like fasting (from food or certain luxuries) and giving to those in need help us detach from material comforts. They cultivate empathy for the marginalized and heighten our awareness of our own spiritual hunger for God.

Silence and Solitude: Taking a few moments each day for silent prayer or meditation can heighten our sensitivity to the Holy Spirit's leading. In a culture rife with constant noise, solitude becomes a radical act of humility, an intentional space to hear God's still, small voice.

Cultivating Supportive Sisterhoods

The spiritual journey was never meant to be a solo endeavor. For Black women, in particular, sisterhood can be a fortress against the storms of life.

Accountability Partners: Find one or two close friends who share your desire for deeper faith. Encourage each other to practice vulnerability, pray for one another's needs, and celebrate victories together.

Small Groups or "Circle Meetings": Many Black churches have a long tradition of women's circles or mission groups. These gatherings can be safe spaces for testimonies, shared prayer, and honest conversation about struggles. If your church doesn't have one, consider starting a weekly or monthly meeting in someone's home or even online.

Mentorship: Seek guidance from seasoned women of faith who can offer wisdom gleaned from years of walking with the Lord. Mentors provide perspective, scriptural grounding, and practical tips on how to balance faith commitments with family, work, and ministry.

Seeking Counsel or Therapy

Acknowledging emotional burdens is a vital part of poverty of spirit. Sometimes we need professional support to process trauma, stress, or anxiety—particularly as Black women who face unique sociocultural pressures. Seeking a Christian counselor or a mental health professional who understands the intersection of race, gender, and faith can be transformative. Therapy is not a sign of spiritual weakness; it is an act of stewardship over the mind and body God has entrusted to us.

Reflective Questions and Journal Prompts

To close this chapter, here are some prompts to help you integrate "Blessed are the poor in spirit" into your daily life. Take a few moments to reflect or journal on each point. Feel free to discuss these questions with a trusted friend, small group, or spiritual mentor.

1. *Where Do I Need God's Help Most?*
   Identify areas in your life—finances, health, relationships, or career—where you often feel overwhelmed. In what ways might inviting God into these spaces bring relief or direction?

2. *How Have I Seen Humility Lead to Breakthrough?*
   Think of a time when admitting your need—either to God or another person—opened the door to greater clarity, provision, or healing. What lessons can you draw from that experience?

3. *How Do I Practice Vulnerability?*

   Is it easy or difficult for you to ask for help, voice your fears, or share your burdens with a community? Why do you think that is? What steps can you take to grow in healthy vulnerability?

4. *Who in My Life Embodies Poverty of Spirit?*

   Consider people you know—elders, friends, or mentors—who exhibit a deep reliance on God. What qualities stand out to you, and how might you cultivate those qualities in your own life?

5. *What Does Solidarity Look Like for Me?*

   Poverty of spirit is not just about personal humility but also about standing with others in need. Are there local organizations, church ministries, or community efforts you can support? In what ways can you leverage your resources—time, finances, talents—to uplift others?

Conclusion

When Jesus proclaims, "Blessed are the poor in spirit," He upends the world's definition of success. Instead of valorizing those who seem to "have it all together," Christ honors those who recognize that every breath, every blessing, and every bit of wisdom ultimately comes from God. For Black women, this recognition can be a healing balm amid societal pressures to always be the "strong one." Embracing our need for God allows us to shatter the myth of invincibility and instead lean on a divine presence that offers rest for our souls (cf. Matthew 11:28—30).

In the next chapters, we will explore more of Jesus' teachings, each revealing a different facet of God's kingdom. From "The Truth Will Set You Free" to "I Have Overcome the World," we'll see how Christ's words intersect with our real-life trials, joys, and aspirations. As you move forward, hold fast to the promise that, indeed, the kingdom of heaven belongs to the poor in spirit—those who dare to be vulnerable enough to receive it.

May you enter this week with a renewed sense of God's nearness, letting go of burdens you were never meant to carry alone. Remember: Your poverty of spirit is not a handicap; it is a holy doorway to grace.

Chapter 2
"The Truth Will Set You Free" (John 8:32)

"Then Jesus said to the Jews who had believed in him, 'If you continue in my word, you are truly my disciples; and you will know the truth, and the truth will make you free.'"
—John 8:31–32 (NRSV)

We live in a world where "truth" can often seem elusive, especially when oppressive systems spin narratives designed to control and suppress. Yet Jesus' words in John 8:32 offer a clear, unwavering promise: *the truth will set you free.* For Black women, whose identities and stories have so often been distorted or dismissed, this passage speaks powerfully to our spiritual and social liberation. It reminds us that God's truth— both in Scripture and in our lived testimonies—holds the power to dismantle lies and embolden us to walk in freedom.

In this chapter, we will explore Jesus' statement within its biblical context and reflect on how embracing God's truth disrupts oppressive structures in our world. We will also consider the role of Womanist Theology, which elevates Black women's experiences and truth-telling as an essential part of our faith journey. Finally, we'll delve into practical applications: how to stand firmly in truth amid workplace challenges, church politics, and societal pressures. We will conclude with accounts of *real* Christian Black women who have found freedom by speaking and living truthfully in Christ.

Biblical Setting

Freedom in Christ: Liberation from Sin and Oppression

Jesus utters the well-known phrase "the truth will make you free" in John 8, during a discourse with Jewish believers and religious leaders. The conversation revolves around what it means to be a true disciple. For Jesus, continuing in His word—aligning life and action with His teaching—reveals divine truth that leads to genuine liberty. While the immediate context addresses liberation from sin, it also resonates with social and political overtones. In the first-century Roman Empire, people faced physical subjugation and institutionalized injustice; they yearned for both political and spiritual freedom.

For us today, freedom in Christ transcends a narrow focus on personal sin to encompass liberation from systemic evils—whether racism, sexism, economic inequality, or other injustices. When Jesus says, "the truth will make you free," He speaks of a transformation that breaks chains both spiritual and societal. This inclusive vision is particularly relevant for Black women, who frequently confront structural barriers and oppressive narratives in daily life.

Worldly "Truths" vs. God's Truth

Throughout history, oppressive powers have wielded distorted "truths" to justify subjugation and maintain control. Such deceptions might appear as racial stereotypes, myths about "inferiority," or even twisted readings of Scripture to defend injustices—like the misuse of the "curse of Ham" to sanction slavery. By contrast, God's truth in Scripture affirms the value and dignity of all people. Galatians 3:28 (NRSV) declares, "There is no longer Jew or Greek, there is no longer slave or free, there is no longer male and female; for all of you are one in Christ Jesus."

This biblical witness makes plain that any claim denying Black women's full humanity or leadership contradicts the essence of the gospel. Jesus' promise of freedom arises from a truth that sees every person as beloved, worthy, and empowered. Embracing such truth is a direct affront to any cultural norms that would marginalize Black women or reduce their God-given identity and gifts.

Liberation Theology Emphasis

Dismantling Structural Injustices

Liberation Theology, with roots in Latin America, asserts that God takes a preferential option for the poor and oppressed. The gospel, it teaches, cannot be fully proclaimed if it fails to confront the systemic forces that dehumanize entire communities. When Jesus promises that truth will set us free, He is not limiting that freedom to internal salvation alone. He also points to the dismantling of oppressive structures, whether political, economic, or social.

For Black women, this perspective resonates profoundly. We encounter systems that undervalue our labor, undercompensate our efforts, and ignore our contributions. Liberation Theology reminds us that embracing the truth of the gospel means challenging these injustices head-on. It is an act of discipleship that requires us to reject the world's false narratives—such as the myth of the "strong Black woman" who must silently endure hardship—and to step into the fullness of our rightful place in God's plan.

Freedom in Christ and Social, Economic, Racial Liberation
The Greek term for "make you free" in John 8:32 implies an active release from captivity. It evokes the image of unbinding chains, both literal and metaphorical. When we root ourselves in Christ's truth, we expose and unravel the lies that keep individuals and communities imprisoned. This liberating truth has concrete implications:

Economic Liberation: God's truth motivates us to advocate for fair wages and combat the racial wealth gap, seeing economic justice as a spiritual matter.

Racial Liberation: Embracing the gospel compels us to confront racism in workplaces, schools, and churches, challenging discriminatory practices or biased policies.

Spiritual Liberation: Strongholds of shame and fear crumble when we grasp the depth of God's love. Prayer, communal worship, and biblical study become gateways to healing generational and individual trauma.

In Liberation Theology, spiritual growth and social transformation are intertwined. When we internalize Jesus' liberating truth, we become agents of change in our families, churches, and communities. We work to align our personal lives—and the broader world—with the equitable, justice-centered values of God's kingdom.

Womanist Insights

Truth-Telling as Resistance
Due to historical and ongoing oppression, many Black communities have learned to safeguard their truths as a form of protection. While prudence and caution can be necessary, long-term secrecy or silence can inadvertently perpetuate oppressive dynamics. Womanist Theology emphasizes that naming abuse, addressing racism and sexism, and shedding light on hidden struggles are spiritual acts of resistance.

Telling the truth—whether through testimony, protest, or interpersonal confrontation—validates our God-given humanity.

It also interrupts a status quo that thrives on our invisibility or complicity. Speaking truth in love can happen in small settings (like family gatherings) or large-scale movements (like public protests or legislative advocacy). In each instance, God meets us in our honest words, bringing clarity and power to break cycles of untruth.

"Stony the Road We Trod": The Power of Our Stories
"Stony the Road We Trod" is a famous line from the hymn "Lift Every Voice and Sing" and also the title of a notable anthology on African American biblical interpretation. It echoes the arduous path Black people have traveled in a society structured by racism. Womanist theologians insist that sharing our lived realities—our personal and collective stories—is vital for both our healing and communal consciousness.

By refusing to accept the silencing of our narratives, we reclaim authority over our histories. Whether in pulpits, classrooms, social media, or written memoirs, the stories of Black women illuminate the ways we have always encountered God in the trenches. They also point us toward freedom yet to be fully realized. Such storytelling honors our ancestors' struggles and strengthens new generations by showing how divine truth operates in the real world.

Practical Application: Owning Our Truth

Boldly Speaking Against Injustice

Workplace Advocacy: Document incidents of discrimination or microaggressions and bring them to the attention of HR when safe. Seek out or establish employee resource groups that address racial and gender disparities. Collaborate with coworkers committed to inclusivity and fairness, pooling resources for greater impact.

Church Engagement: Encourage frank dialogue about racism, sexism, and homophobia within your congregation. Initiate or participate in Bible studies centered on liberation texts (e.g., Exodus, Luke 4:18–19). Press for more inclusive leadership roles, ensuring that women's voices—especially Black women's voices—shape the direction of ministry.

Community Mobilization: Attend and speak at local town halls, school board meetings, or community forums to address systemic issues affecting Black neighborhoods. Partner with advocacy groups or organizations dedicated to racial and gender equity. Support local officials who champion social justice reforms and hold them accountable.

Tools for Personal Growth

Reading Scripture with a Liberation Lens: Approach biblical texts by asking, "Whose voice is missing?" and "How does God respond to the marginalized?" Read works by womanist or

African American biblical scholars to gain fresh perspectives on passages often interpreted through a Eurocentric lens.

Workshops and Discussion Groups: Attend seminars or conferences focusing on racial reconciliation, leadership development, and social justice. Organize or join small groups to discuss books by Black theologians, historians, and activists, fostering deeper understanding and collective action.

Self-Care and Communal Support: Recognize that standing in truth can be draining. Nourish your spirit through prayer, rest, healthy boundaries, and, if needed, professional counseling.
   - Cultivate trusted circles—friend groups, online forums, local gatherings—where you can safely decompress and strategize.

Stories of Freedom

To illustrate the transformative impact of truth-telling, we can look to the lives of *real* Christian Black women who confronted oppressive norms by boldly declaring and living out the gospel truth. Their testimonies remind us that our capacity to challenge injustice is inseparable from our faith in a liberating Christ.

Fannie Lou Hamer

A devout Christian and a key figure in the Civil Rights Movement, Fannie Lou Hamer combined biblical conviction with grassroots activism. Best known for her declaration, "I'm sick and tired of being sick and tired," Hamer spoke unapologetically about the injustices inflicted upon Black

Americans in the Jim Crow South. Her unwavering truth-telling exposed voter suppression, police brutality, and the socio-economic barriers facing Black sharecroppers.

Hamer often referenced her faith, praying and singing gospel songs during protests and meetings. She believed that God's truth mandated full freedom for all people. In 1964, at the Democratic National Convention, her televised testimony about violent voter intimidation shook the nation. Though pressured to remain silent, she persisted, trusting that the truth would vindicate her and strengthen the cause. Her courage continues to inspire those who see faith as integral to social justice.

Pauli Murray

Pauli Murray—an Episcopal priest, civil rights advocate, and legal scholar—was another formidable voice for truth. Murray co-founded the National Organization for Women and championed gender equality in both church and society. By wielding her legal expertise and theological insights, she exposed systemic discrimination that intersected race and gender.

As a Black, queer woman, Murray faced multiple layers of bias within academic institutions and religious communities. Yet she persisted in articulating a Christian ethic that recognized God's love for all marginalized peoples. Her autobiography, *Song in a Weary Throat: An American Pilgrimage*, and her legal writings stand as enduring testaments to the power of owning one's truth—even when that truth challenges the status quo. In 1977, she became the first Black woman ordained as an Episcopal priest, shattering a barrier rooted in centuries of racial and gender exclusion.

Dr. Renita J. Weems

A noted biblical scholar and ordained elder in the African Methodist Episcopal Church, Dr. Renita J. Weems has contributed significantly to Womanist Theology. In works like *Just a Sister Away* and *Listening for God: A Minister's Journey Through Silence and Doubt*, Weems candidly addresses the experiences of Black women navigating faith, relationships, and church life. By engaging Scripture with an ear toward women's lived realities, she shines a light on how patriarchal assumptions can distort biblical interpretation.

Dr. Weems' scholarly and pastoral ministry exemplifies speaking truth to both ecclesial and academic powers that have historically sidelined Black women's voices. Her insistence on centering Black women's experiences as legitimate biblical hermeneutics challenges the notion that theology must cater to Eurocentric or male-dominated standards. Through teaching, preaching, and writing, Weems models how owning our truth in Christ can lead to personal and communal liberation.

Reflective Questions and Journal Prompts

1. *Personal vs. Structural Truth*

When you hear Jesus say, "The truth will set you free," do you instinctively think about personal issues (e.g., sin, guilt) or social/structural problems (e.g., racism, sexism)? How might God's truth address both realms?

2. *Unmasking Cultural Lies*

    Identify one harmful narrative about Black women that you've encountered in media, education, or church settings. How can Scripture and personal testimony dismantle that falsehood?

3. *Speaking Truth in Love*

    Think of a time when you confronted a difficult situation (workplace bias, family conflict) with honesty rather than silence. What did you learn about courage and compassion?

4. *Barriers to Embracing Truth*

    Sometimes we resist truth because it challenges our comfort zones. Are there any truths about your own life or community you find hard to accept? How might Jesus' promise of freedom encourage you to face them?

5. *Testimony and Collective Change*

    Recall a moment when sharing your personal story or hearing another's testimony led to positive change. What does this suggest about the power of collective truth-telling in your church or local community?

Conclusion

In John 8:32, Jesus' declaration that "the truth will make you free" stands as a promise that resonates across time and culture. For Black women, who face the compounded weight of racial and gender oppression, owning and proclaiming truth is both a spiritual discipline and a pathway to liberation. As Fannie Lou Hamer, Pauli Murray, and Renita Weems demonstrate, trusting God's word involves far more than personal piety; it calls us to unmask injustice, advocate for the marginalized, and reshape institutions to reflect God's justice and love.

Whether you are challenging workplace inequities, leading a church Bible study on racial reconciliation, or simply sharing your personal story, remember that *truth has power*. It shines a light on hidden realities, breaks oppressive chains, and reaffirms that we are all made in the image of a liberating God. Lean into Christ's assurance that your sincere pursuit of truth—rooted in Scripture, guided by the Holy Spirit, and expressed in community—will lead you into profound freedom.

As you move forward, consider the practical strategies outlined in this chapter—speaking up against injustice, reading Scripture through a liberation lens, and drawing strength from supportive networks. May your resolve to embody truth in every sphere of your life bring you closer to God, to yourself, and to the community you serve. In a world awash with distortions, Christ's liberating truth remains our firm foundation, enabling us to stand tall and bear witness to the freedom that is ours in Him.

Chapter 3
"Love Your Enemies" (Matthew 5:44)

"But I say to you, Love your enemies and pray for those who persecute you…"
—Matthew 5:44 (NRSV)

Few commands of Jesus are as challenging—or as transformative—as "Love your enemies." Located in the heart of the Sermon on the Mount, this instruction defies conventional wisdom. Human nature often dictates retaliation or avoidance when confronted with opposition, especially the vicious kind rooted in racial hostility and gender oppression. Yet Jesus dares us to resist hate by embodying a radical love—a love that surpasses personal comfort and extends toward those who stand against us.

For Black women, this directive is particularly poignant. We have inherited a legacy of intersecting forms of injustice: from slavery and Jim Crow to contemporary systemic racism, misogynoir, and economic marginalization. Still, within this crucible of oppression, many Black women have birthed a resilience infused with grace, a capacity to answer hostility with the kind of love that sets communities on a new path. This chapter explores the complexity of "loving our enemies," highlighting how it coexists with boundaries, self-care, and active resistance against oppression. We will also discuss historical and present-day examples of Black women (and the broader Black Church tradition) that demonstrate love as a force more potent than hate.

Radical Call to Love
Situating the Teaching in the Sermon on the Mount
The Sermon on the Mount (Matthew 5–7) is a blueprint of God's kingdom ethics: humility, mercy, righteousness, and a commitment to peace that subverts the status quo. In Matthew 5:43–48, Jesus contrasts the well-known injunction, "You shall love your neighbor and hate your enemy," with His revolutionary admonition to *love* one's enemies and *pray* for those who persecute. He concludes by urging His listeners to "be perfect... as your heavenly Father is perfect" (Matthew 5:48, NRSV).

The Greek term often translated as "perfect" (teleios) can also convey maturity or completeness. This suggests that loving our enemies is a hallmark of spiritual maturity—a sign that we grasp God's expansive grace. By situating this teaching in a sermon that pronounces blessings upon the meek, the poor in spirit, and the peacemakers, Jesus declares that the "common sense" approach of returning evil for evil is incompatible with the righteousness of God's reign.

Acknowledging the Difficulty Amid Racial Hostility and Gender Oppression
No discussion of "loving our enemies" would be honest without acknowledging how difficult and, at times, painful this

command can be—especially for Black women. Generations have endured racial slurs, workplace discrimination, physical threats, and even violence. Meanwhile, many also face gender-specific injustices within and beyond Black communities. When Jesus calls us to love our persecutors, it can feel not only unreasonable but potentially harmful if misunderstood to mean acquiescence.

Yet Jesus does not advocate for passivity in the face of evil. Rather, He points to a love powerful enough to disrupt hate's cycle. One might think of it as holy defiance: we refuse to let our enemies define us, trap us in bitterness, or block us from God's transformative grace. Even as we lament injustice, pursue legal redress, or organize protests, we do so without succumbing to hatred that corrodes the spirit. This tension—loving one's enemies while resisting oppression—stands at the heart of the Christian ethic.

Womanist Theology and Self-Love

"Love Your Enemies" Does Not Mean Passive Acceptance of Abuse

Womanist theologians highlight the importance of reading Scripture in ways that honor the lived experiences of Black women. A superficial reading of "love your enemies" can leave survivors of abuse feeling guilt-ridden, as though they must endure mistreatment in order to be Christlike. However, womanist interpretations push back against such misuse of the text, emphasizing that *godly love is never an endorsement of harm.*

In the same Sermon on the Mount, Jesus condemns forms of violence and exploitation, underscoring that His discipleship ethic is rooted in justice and compassion (Matthew 5:21–26, 5:38–42). To love one's enemies, in this light, is to actively seek both personal wholeness and the potential redemption of the oppressor. It does *not* entail silent suffering or a lack of accountability.

Protecting Oneself and Practicing Self-Care
Central to womanist theology is the affirmation of Black women's inherent worth, challenging any theological stance that would have us perpetually sacrifice ourselves to the point of erasure. Self-care is thus a spiritual discipline, a necessary boundary that protects our bodies, minds, and spirits.

Loving enemies does not contradict prudent self-protection. In fact, healthy boundaries—physical, emotional, spiritual— become the soil in which genuine love can grow. If we remain trapped in environments of constant harm, we cannot fully embody Christ's reconciling mission. God does not require us to stay in unsafe or abusive relationships to prove our forgiveness or "love." We can practice compassion while also drawing clear lines that shield our well-being and that of our community.

Resistance Through Love

Lessons from the Civil Rights Movement

A vibrant example of love as both resistance and moral power is found in the Civil Rights Movement. Dr. Martin Luther King Jr. preached a "theology of love" that drew from Jesus' teachings, particularly Matthew 5:44 and Luke 6:27–36. He believed that "unearned suffering" could be redemptive, if channeled through nonviolent protest and radical forgiveness. While Dr. King is often the public face of this movement, Black women were essential architects and sustainers of this ethic.

From **Septima Clark**, who championed citizenship schools that taught literacy and civic engagement, to **Diane Nash**, who helped organize the Freedom Rides, Black women embodied sacrificial yet empowering love. They faced harassment, beatings, and jailing, yet many continued to insist on the humanity of their oppressors—without relinquishing their own dignity. Their commitment to nonviolence was not weakness but a fierce strategy that exposed the brutality of segregation and won sympathizers nationwide.

Love as a Tactic for Dismantling Hate and Fear

Hate thrives on dehumanization. Once we view someone as less than human, it becomes easier to justify violence against them. Conversely, love humanizes both the self and the other—forcing an acknowledgment of shared dignity. This was a key insight of the Civil Rights Movement and remains a potent tactic today.

In everyday life, "enemy love" might manifest in simpler ways. We might challenge coworkers or neighbors who harbor racist or sexist attitudes, not by mirroring their hostility, but by calmly stating the truth about our shared humanity and refusing to stoop to hateful language. Though difficult, such an approach can erode stereotypes and plant seeds for transformation. Love's long game—patient yet unyielding—often succeeds where aggression fails, because it appeals to the conscience, the better angels of human nature.

Practical Tools

Healthy Boundaries: Distinguishing Between Righteous Reconciliation and Enabling Harm

Identify the Nature of the Conflict: Not all "enemy" relationships are equal. Sometimes, the conflict stems from a misunderstanding or implicit bias; at other times, it involves clear, ongoing abuse. True reconciliation is impossible if harm goes unaddressed. Thus, the first step is recognizing whether the enemy is open to dialogue and change or entrenched in destructive behavior.

Communicate Clear Expectations: Loving your enemy does not equate to remaining silent about disrespect or harm. If someone consistently undermines or threatens you, articulate the boundaries you need. This can involve stating: "I cannot allow you to speak to me that way," or "If this behavior continues, I will remove myself from the situation."

Seek Wise Counsel: Consult mentors, friends, therapists, or spiritual leaders for guidance. Sometimes we need a trustworthy external perspective to determine how best to navigate a fraught relationship. This is especially crucial if the situation involves potential legal or safety concerns.

Evaluate the Possibility of Reconciliation: True reconciliation requires the offender to acknowledge wrongdoing and commit to meaningful change. Where these elements are absent, forcing a relationship may only perpetuate harm. Still, letting go of hatred remains essential for *your* spiritual freedom.

Prayer and Meditation Practices

Centering Prayer: Spend a few minutes each day in silent meditation, inviting God's presence to soften your heart. Focus on a simple phrase or Scripture, such as "Lord, teach me to love." This practice can help ground you when hurt or anger flare.

Prayers of Intercession: In Matthew 5:44, Jesus specifically calls us to *pray* for those who persecute us. This doesn't mean endorsing their actions but rather entrusting the situation to God's transformative power. Praying for an enemy can shift our perspective, reminding us that this person, too, is within God's reach.

Journaling Forgiveness: When anger lingers, try writing down your thoughts about the person or circumstance that wounded you. Then, alongside those words, list any areas where you see potential for grace, or where you sense God nudging you to release bitterness. Over time, this practice can reveal internal shifts toward compassion or acceptance.

Communal Worship and Lament: Gather with fellow believers who understand your journey—perhaps in a small group dedicated to healing or a prayer circle in your church. Share your struggles and invite the community to intercede for you and the person(s) who have caused harm. Collective lament and mutual support can offer solace and clarity.

Community Engagement

Facilitating Dialogue in Divided Communities or Workplaces

"Love your enemies" takes on urgent relevance in communities fractured by political, racial, or ideological divisions. Black women often find themselves in the role of mediator or peacemaker, whether in the workplace, the local church, or civic groups. Yet stepping into this role must be discerned carefully; it should not be an expectation that Black women alone shoulder the emotional burden of reconciliation.

Practical Steps:

Organize Listening Circles: Create a structured space where individuals share personal experiences regarding race, gender, or conflict. Each participant speaks without interruption, fostering empathy and reducing the temptation to demonize "the other side."

Encourage Shared Initiatives: Collaborate on community projects—neighborhood cleanups, food drives, or mentoring programs—that bring diverse groups together around a common goal. Practical cooperation often builds relational bridges that discussion alone cannot.

Promote Fair Representation: Ensure that voices from marginalized groups, especially Black women, hold leadership positions in dialogues. Authentic healing requires centering those most affected by prejudice and hostility.

Activism and Advocacy Rooted in Love, Not Bitterness
Activism is frequently fueled by righteous anger—a response to systemic harm. While anger can be productive in highlighting injustice, it risks devolving into bitterness if not tempered by love. Martin Luther King Jr. warned against allowing our moral indignation to curdle into hatred, lest we become what we oppose. For Black women, who often organize at the front lines of social movements, nurturing a spirit of love can sustain our activism over the long haul.

Rallying for Policy Change: Love compels us to care for those most vulnerable, shaping our legislative goals—whether expanding voting rights, advocating for fair housing, or ensuring reproductive justice.

Mentorship and Education: Offer workshops on nonviolent communication, conflict resolution, or race/gender awareness. These efforts multiply the influence of love-based activism by equipping others to approach social issues with empathy and firmness.

Sustained Self-Care: One act of revolutionary love is caring for our own mental, emotional, and spiritual health, ensuring that bitterness does not take root. From counseling to sabbaticals, rest is a necessary component of sustained advocacy.

Reflective Questions and Journal Prompts

1. *Defining 'Enemy'*

   Who or what do you perceive as an "enemy" in your life—an individual, an unjust system, or a harmful cultural narrative? How does naming that enemy affect your approach to it?

2. *Healthy Boundaries vs. Passive Acceptance*

   How can you practice self-protection while still seeking to love those who have harmed you? Can you think of specific boundaries that affirm your dignity and safety?

3. *Historical Inspiration*

   Consider a figure from the Civil Rights Movement or your own community who embodied "enemy love." What aspects of their story resonate with you, and what strategies might you adopt in your own conflicts?

4. *Overcoming Bitterness*

Where in your life do you sense bitterness or resentment taking hold? What prayer practices or supportive relationships could help you nurture forgiveness or healing?

5. *Love in Action*

Jesus' command to love enemies often translates into real-world activism (marches, petitions, dialogues). How might you engage in a tangible act of love toward someone or something you currently deem hostile?

Conclusion

"Love your enemies" is a command that pushes us beyond the boundaries of conventional morality, inviting us to participate in the subversive logic of God's kingdom. For Black women—who routinely face racism, sexism, and countless forms of hostility—this teaching can appear impractical or even dangerous if interpreted superficially. Yet Jesus does not call us to submit passively to evil; rather, He calls us to disarm hatred with a love so resilient that it transcends personal vendettas, forging a path toward justice and possible reconciliation.

Womanist theology helps us discern that loving our enemies includes loving ourselves, refusing to tolerate abuse, and creating boundaries that foster spiritual growth. By examining historical movements like the Civil Rights era, we learn that love can be a formidable strategy of resistance—amplifying the moral stakes for oppressors while protecting our own humanity.

Moving forward, consider the practical tools outlined here: set firm boundaries, pray for those who harm you, and cultivate a posture of compassionate resistance. Embrace community engagement that fosters dialogue and activism without succumbing to enmity. In doing so, you join a long lineage of Black women who have wielded divine love to break cycles of hostility and guide entire communities toward healing. Ultimately, this love—both tender and unyielding—reflects the heart of a God who meets us in our pain and empowers us to transcend it, carrying forward the hope of restoration for every wounded place.

Chapter 4
"Seek First the Kingdom of God"
(Matthew 6:33)

"But strive first for the kingdom of God and his righteousness, and all these things will be given to you as well."
—Matthew 6:33 (NRSV)

In a world that constantly demands our time, energy, and devotion, Jesus' call to "seek first the kingdom of God" (Matthew 6:33) can feel both inspiring and challenging. Whether it's juggling careers, caring for family, or pursuing our passions, Black women are often asked to carry multiple, overlapping responsibilities. Amid these pressures, it can be easy for spiritual priorities to slip into the margins of our busy lives. Yet Jesus' words remind us that true flourishing emerges when God's reign becomes our central pursuit. This chapter explores what it means to seek God's kingdom—biblically, theologically, and in practical, everyday terms.

Prioritizing God's Reign

Biblical and Theological Foundations
In the Gospel of Matthew, Jesus frequently speaks of the "kingdom of heaven" or "kingdom of God," describing it in parables and direct teachings. Far from being a distant or purely spiritual realm, this kingdom is God's dynamic rule entering into human history. It is both already among us—through

48

Christ's presence and the work of the Holy Spirit—and not yet
fully realized, as we still await the complete restoration of
creation.

When Jesus instructs His followers to "strive first for the
kingdom of God" in the Sermon on the Mount, He positions
God's reign as the primary lens through which we make
decisions. This is not about escaping daily life or ignoring real-
world problems. Rather, it is about letting God's values shape
how we approach every concern—from the mundane (food,
clothing) to the profound (justice, mercy). By placing God at the
center, we discover a new orientation that elevates love,
compassion, righteousness, and community above self-serving
interests.

Justice, Righteousness, and Mercy as Kingdom Values
Biblically, the kingdom of God is often associated with
righteousness (dikaiosynē in Greek), which encompasses both
ethical conduct and just relationships. This means that the
kingdom is not only about personal morality but also about how
society treats its most vulnerable members. For instance, the
prophets of the Old Testament repeatedly call Israel to embody
mercy and justice toward orphans, widows, and foreigners (cf.
Micah 6:8, Isaiah 1:17). Jesus echoes this prophetic tradition by
caring for the poor, the sick, and those deemed "unclean" by
religious norms.

For Black women—whose communities often face systemic discrimination—seeking the kingdom involves advocating for a world where resources and opportunities are more equitably distributed, and where the dignity of every person is upheld. By centering justice, righteousness, and mercy, we align our lives with God's reign, allowing divine priorities to inform both our personal choices and our larger social commitments.

Liberation-Centered Kingdom Vision

God's Kingdom as a Social Reality

Liberation Theology teaches us that the gospel cannot be separated from social, political, and economic realities. In this view, the kingdom of God is not just a distant hope; it is a present force dismantling oppression and lifting up the marginalized. Throughout the Gospels, Jesus proclaims good news to the poor and declares freedom to the captives (Luke 4:18–19). His miracles—feeding the hungry, healing the sick— demonstrate that God's reign directly confronts systems of scarcity and exclusion.

For Black women, understanding the kingdom of God as a social reality means recognizing that our activism, advocacy, and community-building efforts are deeply spiritual. Supporting fair housing initiatives, mentoring youth, or championing healthcare reforms can be expressions of seeking God's kingdom, because they challenge unjust structures and open avenues for collective flourishing. Indeed, as Martin Luther King Jr. once argued, "Any religion that professes to be concerned about the souls of people and is not concerned about the slums that damn them... is a spiritually moribund religion."

Womanist Theology's Emphasis on Holistic Flourishing
Womanist Theology adds another layer, emphasizing that God's kingdom touches every facet of Black women's lives—our bodies, emotions, relationships, and communities. Womanist scholars like Jacquelyn Grant and Delores Williams argue that spiritual wholeness is incomplete if it neglects our day-to-day struggles with racism, sexism, and classism. Thus, seeking first the kingdom also involves affirming our God-given worth, resisting stereotypes, and nurturing spaces where Black women can thrive without apology.

Holistic flourishing includes self-care, educational attainment, creative expression, and entrepreneurial endeavors, among many other pursuits. Each of these can be integrated into a kingdom vision when guided by love, justice, and mutual uplift. Far from being self-centered, caring for ourselves and our sisters in Christ aligns with the biblical mandate to "love your neighbor as yourself" (Matthew 22:39). When we live in full awareness of God's liberating presence, we see each domain of life—personal, communal, spiritual—as intertwined threads in the tapestry of God's kingdom.

Everyday Priorities

Aligning Personal Goals with God's Priorities

For many Black women, faith has always been the wellspring of endurance and hope. Yet in the midst of survival, it is easy to lose sight of how our individual aims can reflect kingdom values. Seeking first the kingdom means we consciously weave godly principles into our goal-setting:

Volunteering: Dedicate some of your gifts and time to serve in a local ministry or community outreach. Whether tutoring young girls in math or visiting elderly church members, these acts of service embody God's love in tangible ways.

Mentoring: Pass on your professional or spiritual wisdom to younger Black women, empowering them to navigate societal barriers. Such mentorship mirrors the relational aspect of God's kingdom, where no one is left to journey alone.

Community Building: Partner with neighbors, church members, or local organizations to host events like health fairs, voter registration drives, or Bible study groups that address social challenges. By fostering communal solidarity, we enact the unity Jesus prayed for in John 17.

Career, Finances, and Family Decisions

Career: Whether you are a corporate executive, educator, artist, or entrepreneur, seeking God's kingdom means discerning how your professional path can serve divine purposes. You might ask: "Does this job allow me to advocate for justice?" or "Am I able to use my position to create opportunities for others?" These questions ensure that success is measured not just by salary or status but by kingdom impact.

Finances: Financial stewardship is another dimension of kingdom living. While saving for the future is wise, hoarding resources without regard for those in need can contradict the biblical ethic of generosity. Consider allocating a portion of your income—beyond tithes—to causes that uplift marginalized communities, whether through scholarships, social enterprises, or church programs geared toward economic empowerment.

Family: Balancing familial responsibilities with kingdom priorities can be delicate. Seeking first the kingdom does not mean neglecting our loved ones; it means modeling faith and justice within our households. Praying together, serving others as a family, and discussing social issues openly with children can instill values that endure across generations. In this way, the family itself becomes an outpost of God's kingdom, nurturing hearts committed to compassion and integrity.

Balancing Commitments

Practical Time-Management Tools
Black women often juggle multiple roles—provider, caregiver, church leader, community volunteer—leaving us susceptible to burnout. A crucial aspect of seeking first the kingdom is learning

to steward our time so that we can sustain our commitments without sacrificing our well-being. Consider these tools:

Prioritized To-Do Lists: At the start of each week, list tasks in order of importance. Place kingdom-centered activities—prayer, Bible study, service—near the top, ensuring they don't get squeezed out by life's busyness.

Time Blocking: Allocate specific time slots for work, family, rest, and spiritual practices. By treating spiritual and community commitments as non-negotiable appointments, you signal their importance to yourself and others.

Setting Realistic Goals: Avoid overcommitment by assessing how much you can reasonably handle in any given season. Remember, Jesus often withdrew to pray and rest (Luke 5:16). Emulating His rhythm of engagement and solitude helps preserve our emotional and spiritual health.

Learning to Say "No"

Saying "yes" to every request can leave us exhausted and unable to focus on what God most wants us to do. Empower yourself to say "no"—even to worthy endeavors—if they would detract from your primary calling or well-being. This discernment is part of seeking God's kingdom: it honors the fact that we are finite beings, reliant on God's strength and wisdom rather than our own endless striving.

Setting boundaries can sometimes feel counter-cultural, especially if you're used to being the "go-to" person in family or church circles. But boundaries protect your capacity to serve joyfully, preventing resentment and burnout. Prayerfully weigh each opportunity, asking: "Does this invitation align with the gifts and direction God has placed in my life right now?" If the answer is no, trust that God will raise up others to fill that role.

Stories of Alignment

Examples of Black Women Prioritizing God's Call

Seeking first the kingdom of God has taken countless forms in the lives of Black Christian women across history. For instance, Ida B. Wells, an investigative journalist and early civil rights leader, was motivated by her Christian faith to expose the horrors of lynching. She balanced her family life—becoming one of the first Black women to keep her own last name after marriage—with relentless advocacy for racial justice. Wells' dedication shows that neither motherhood nor a busy professional life negates a calling to fight oppression; rather, these dimensions can enrich our testimony when anchored in kingdom values.

Another example is Prathia Hall, a civil rights activist and Baptist preacher who worked alongside Dr. Martin Luther King Jr. Hall's theological convictions informed her activism; she viewed the struggle for civil rights as an outworking of God's kingdom. Despite facing sexism within and outside the church, she continued preaching and organizing, believing that God's reign demanded freedom and dignity for all. Her life illustrates how a commitment to justice can flourish alongside pastoral and community responsibilities, reflecting a holistic vision of discipleship.

The "Proverbs 31 Woman" in Modern Context

The famed "Proverbs 31 woman" is often cited as a biblical portrait of a virtuous wife and mother. Traditionally, she's described as industrious, charitable, and wise—qualities that remain relevant. However, some modern readers find the passage overwhelming or unrealistic. Does "seeking wool and flax" (Proverbs 31:13) translate to crocheting in the 21st century? Must every woman rise at dawn to prepare food (v. 15)?

A kingdom-centered reading of Proverbs 31 emphasizes principles rather than rigid prescriptions. For instance:

- **Industriousness** can be reimagined as using your gifts—entrepreneurial, creative, or intellectual—to bless your household and community.

- **Generosity** involves extending resources to the poor, supporting causes of justice, and nurturing the next generation.

- **Wisdom** means consulting the Holy Spirit and seasoned counsel before making decisions that affect your family, finances, or ministry.

Black women today can embody the spirit of the Proverbs 31 woman by being resourceful, community-minded, and open to God's leading. Rather than trying to replicate an ancient household model, we glean its timeless virtues: integrity, compassion, diligence, and an unshakeable confidence in God.

Reflective Questions and Journal Prompts

1. *Defining God's Kingdom*

   When you imagine God's kingdom, what qualities stand out— justice, peace, joy, community? How do these differ from cultural definitions of success or accomplishment?

2. *Spiritual vs. Societal Transformation*

   In what ways do you see "seeking the kingdom" as both a personal spiritual endeavor and a call to transform oppressive social structures?

3. *Balancing Priorities*

   Reflect on your weekly schedule. Which commitments align with kingdom values, and which ones feel like distractions or burdens? How can you reorient your time toward what truly matters?

4. *Facing Scarcity Mentalities*

   Many Black women have been taught to operate in "survival mode." What fears prevent you from taking bold steps of faith or stepping into leadership? How might kingdom-centered thinking shift your perspective?

5. *Community Building*

Seeking God's kingdom isn't a solo task. Who are the people walking alongside you (friends, mentors, small-group members)? How can you better collaborate and share resources to amplify kingdom impact?

Conclusion

Matthew 6:33, "strive first for the kingdom of God and his righteousness," is not a superficial command; it's an invitation into a radically different way of life. By placing God at the center, we gain clarity about what truly matters—justice, mercy, and communal flourishing—and we learn to allocate our time, energy, and resources accordingly. For Black women, whose burdens are often heavy and schedules stretched thin, this kingdom focus can be both liberating and empowering. It offers a framework where our commitments—whether at home, in the workplace, or on the front lines of social activism—are infused with divine purpose.

Embracing this call requires practical wisdom—learning when to say "yes" and when to say "no," discerning how to invest our gifts, and staying rooted in prayer and fellowship. It also necessitates a courageous vision, one that dares to believe our careers, finances, and relationships can reflect God's reign on earth. As you consider ways to "seek first the kingdom," remember the examples of Ida B. Wells, Prathia Hall, and many unnamed sisters who have persevered in faith, justice, and love. Their stories remind us that God's kingdom is not merely a future hope but a present reality we can build, step by step, decision by decision, with the Holy Spirit guiding us toward abundant life for all.

Chapter 5

"The Spirit of the Lord Is upon Me" (Luke 4:18-19)

"When he came to Nazareth, where he had been brought up, he went to the synagogue on the sabbath day, as was his custom. He stood up to read, and the scroll of the prophet Isaiah was given to him. He unrolled the scroll and found the place where it was written:

'The Spirit of the Lord is upon me,

because he has anointed me

to bring good news to the poor.

He has sent me to proclaim release to the captives

and recovery of sight to the blind,

to let the oppressed go free,

to proclaim the year of the Lord's favor.'"

—Luke 4:16–19 (NRSV)

In Luke 4:18–19, Jesus declares His mission with startling clarity. Reading from the scroll of Isaiah in his hometown synagogue, He aligns Himself with a prophetic tradition that emphasizes liberation, healing, and renewal. For Black women today, this passage remains a powerful testament to God's concern for the marginalized—and a reminder that we, too, are invited into the Spirit's anointing. This chapter delves into the profound implications of Jesus' "mission statement," exploring how it shapes our understanding of liberation theology and womanist empowerment, and offering practical ways we can continue proclaiming freedom in our own contexts.

Jesus' Mission Statement

The Significance of Jesus Reading Isaiah

Luke situates this dramatic event at the beginning of Jesus' public ministry. Having been baptized by John and tested in the wilderness, Jesus returns to Galilee "filled with the power of the Spirit" (Luke 4:14 NRSV). His reading of Isaiah 61 in the synagogue is no random selection; it intentionally announces the nature of His vocation. By choosing these verses, Jesus reveals that His ministry will focus on those typically overlooked by religious and political elites: the poor, the captives, the blind, and the oppressed.

This declaration is all the more striking because it occurs in Nazareth—His hometown—where people knew Jesus as Joseph's son, the carpenter's boy. His proclamation disrupts their familiarity with Him, challenging them to see Him as the Anointed One who brings good news to those society deems unworthy. For us today, this same challenge persists: Are we willing to recognize God's liberating power at work through those we think we already "know"? Will we allow this radical message to reshape our comfort zones and move us toward active engagement in the struggles of marginalized communities?

Linking the Spirit's Anointing with Serving the Marginalized

Jesus' identity as the Messiah is intertwined with a call to serve the oppressed. In ancient Israel, anointing with oil signified setting someone apart for a sacred task—often kingship or priestly service. Here, the anointing by the Holy Spirit specifically equips Jesus to bring release and restoration. This underscores a crucial biblical principle: divine calling is never an abstraction. It is always connected to concrete acts of compassion and justice.

For Black women, this resonates with our lived realities. Many of us have experienced the Spirit's power in intimate ways— through fervent prayer circles, spontaneous worship, or personal devotion. Yet the biblical witness reminds us that any authentic move of the Spirit compels us beyond ourselves, directing our gifts and energies toward healing social wounds. The anointing, therefore, is not merely a private blessing but a public mandate to comfort the afflicted, confront injustice, and embody the gospel in real-world contexts.

Liberation Mandate

Setting Captives Free and Proclaiming Good News

Liberation Theology has long highlighted Luke 4:18–19 as the cornerstone of Jesus' mission to liberate the oppressed. Gustavo Gutiérrez, one of Liberation Theology's pioneers, emphasized that the gospel demands both spiritual conversion and socio-political transformation. From his perspective, Jesus' reference to "bringing good news to the poor" cannot be detached from material realities. It implies systemic change—addressing hunger, inequality, and denial of basic human rights.

For Black women in the United States, the need for liberation intersects multiple dimensions. While spiritual renewal is vital, so is the dismantling of racist, sexist, and classist structures. *Captivity* might look like discriminatory hiring practices, underfunded schools, or lack of access to quality healthcare. *Release* may involve policy reforms, community organizing, and continued advocacy for racial justice. Thus, proclaiming good news to the poor is not limited to evangelistic campaigns; it also entails standing with the marginalized in the pursuit of equity and dismantling whatever systems hold people captive.

Current Issues Affecting Black Women

Jesus' mission statement speaks poignantly to modern realities, including those that disproportionately impact Black women:

Mass Incarceration: Black women are incarcerated at nearly twice the rate of white women, often due to systemic biases and discriminatory policing. The fallout extends beyond prison walls—families are torn apart, economic futures stall, and entire communities suffer from under-resourcing. Proclaiming release to the captives, in this context, may mean supporting prison reform, advocating for restorative justice, or volunteering in re-entry programs.

Healthcare Disparities: From higher maternal mortality rates to reduced access to quality mental health care, Black women frequently face health challenges rooted in systemic neglect. The biblical call to "recovery of sight to the blind" can metaphorically encompass healing in all its forms. Supporting policy changes, raising awareness about healthcare injustices, and providing direct care through church clinics or educational workshops are modern manifestations of Jesus' healing ministry.

Economic Inequality: Wage gaps and underemployment compound the struggles of many Black women. Fighting these disparities aligns with Jesus' mission to uplift the poor. Practical steps might include financial literacy programs in local churches, pushing for legislation that ensures equal pay, and mentoring young women to negotiate salaries and seek entrepreneurial opportunities.

Womanist Empowerment

The Empowering Work of the Holy Spirit Through Black Women's Leadership

Womanist Theology recognizes that the Holy Spirit does not bypass the lived experiences of Black women but meets us right in the thick of our struggles. Throughout history, Black women have acted as spiritual powerhouses within their communities, whether officially ordained or not. They have organized prayer revivals, ministered to neighbors, and led social justice campaigns—often without institutional recognition.

This grassroots leadership exemplifies the Spirit's anointing at work. Harriet Tubman, often called "Moses" for leading enslaved people to freedom, attributed her success to divine visions and guidance. Ella Baker, a behind-the-scenes strategist in the Civil Rights Movement, cultivated young leaders like those in the Student Nonviolent Coordinating Committee (SNCC), modeling a form of ministry that merges spiritual conviction with collective empowerment.

Their contributions validate that the Spirit's power flows most profoundly when we move beyond hierarchies and gatekeeping. As Paul writes, "To each is given the manifestation of the Spirit for the common good" (1 Corinthians 12:7 NRSV). Black women's leadership—whether as pastors, deacons, activists, or Sunday school teachers—reveals how the Holy Spirit can transform oppressive circumstances into platforms for liberation.

Celebrating Women Shaping Spiritual and Social Movements

Across denominations and organizations, Black women continue to shape movements that blend worship, advocacy, and care. Consider the National Council of Negro Women, founded by Mary McLeod Bethune, or various women's ministries in the Black Church that sponsor youth programs, food pantries, and scholarship funds. These efforts go beyond charity; they challenge structures that perpetuate injustice while providing tangible resources to those in need.

In recent decades, women like Dr. Renita J. Weems, Dr. Teresa L. Fry Brown, and Dr. Yolanda Pierce have enriched theological scholarship, bridging academic study with practical church ministry. Their works affirm that the Holy Spirit speaks through Black women's voices, experiences, and perspectives, inviting the broader Christian community to embrace a more inclusive vision of leadership and spiritual authority.

Practical Ways to Proclaim Freedom

Community Initiatives

If we take Jesus' mission seriously, we cannot limit our faith to Sunday morning worship. Below are some community-based strategies for proclaiming freedom in the spirit of Luke 4:18–19:

Prison Ministry: Coordinate visits and Bible studies at local jails or prisons, particularly women's facilities that often lack robust programming. Advocate for sentencing reform and the restoration of voting rights for formerly incarcerated individuals. Provide resources—such as hygiene products and educational materials—to address the material needs of those behind bars.

Homeless Outreach: Organize a rotating shelter program in partnership with other congregations. Offer safe overnight accommodations, meals, and access to job placement resources. Facilitate "life skills" workshops that cover budgeting, résumé building, and self-care.

Youth Mentorship: Develop mentorship programs for teenage girls, pairing them with women who can guide them academically, professionally, and spiritually. Launch creative arts initiatives, sports leagues, or after-school tutoring designed to foster a sense of belonging and self-worth.

"Freedom Circles" and Bible Studies

Congregations can create "freedom circles"—small groups dedicated to exploring Scripture in the context of social justice. These circles might focus on:

- *Biblical Analysis:* Studying passages like Luke 4:18–19, Exodus, or the prophets to understand how God's liberating purposes unfold throughout Scripture.

- *Contemporary Issues:* Linking biblical themes to topics such as voting rights, healthcare disparities, education reform, or climate justice.

- *Action Plans:* Encouraging participants to develop tangible community projects—whether it's advocating at city council meetings or organizing prayer vigils for victims of violence.

In such settings, members can share testimonies, hold one another accountable, and collectively discern where the Spirit is calling them to serve. This communal approach to Scripture transforms Bible study from a purely intellectual exercise into a launching pad for kingdom-inspired action.

Rituals of Anointing

Liturgical Practices Acknowledging the Spirit's Presence

Throughout African American church traditions, the act of anointing with oil has served as a powerful symbol of the Holy Spirit's presence and the believer's consecration to God. Whether performed during healing services, ordinations, or moments of intercessory prayer, the anointing conveys the idea that God's Spirit equips us for the work at hand—just as it did for Jesus.

Some churches practice "consecration services," where leaders or laypeople are anointed for specific ministries: preaching, singing, teaching, activism, or counseling. Others hold regular prayer gatherings where oil is applied as a sign of God's protective, empowering grace. These ceremonies can be deeply moving, connecting believers to the biblical tradition of prophets and apostles who recognized the Spirit's tangible action in physical elements.

The Symbolism of Anointing in African American Church Traditions

Historically, anointing has held extra resonance in Black communities who have faced systematic disenfranchisement. To anoint someone is to declare them chosen, esteemed, and beloved by God—no matter what society says. It stands against narratives of unworthiness, reminding the congregation that the Holy Spirit overrides human hierarchies and prejudices.

In many African American contexts, the anointing also intersects with cultural practices that emphasize touch, call-and-response, and communal affirmation. A person receiving anointing might hear supportive shouts of "Amen!" or "Glory!" from the pews, underscoring that the Spirit's blessing is a shared celebration. This communal aspect is crucial; the gift of anointing is not an individual badge of honor but a collective affirmation that one's talents and voice are vital to the body of Christ.

Through such rituals, believers receive a sacred charge to go into the world—be it the neighborhood school board, the local non-profit, or the broader public square—and proclaim release for the captives, recovery of sight for the blind, and the year of the Lord's favor. In essence, the anointing is not merely a static ceremony; it propels us outward, reinforcing that the same Spirit who empowered Jesus now empowers us to continue His liberating work.

Reflective Questions and Journal Prompts

1. *Personal Anointing*

   Jesus connects the Spirit's anointing to tangible acts of liberation. Where do you sense the Holy Spirit anointing you to bring healing or freedom—within your church, your workplace, or your broader community?

2. *Solidarity with the Oppressed*

Reflect on specific oppressions affecting Black women today: mass incarceration, healthcare disparities, pay inequities. In what ways can you apply Luke 4:18–19 to these modern contexts?

3. *Gifts and Callings*
   Identify one spiritual gift or passion you possess (e.g., administration, teaching, advocacy). How might you use it to fulfill Jesus' mission of setting captives free?

4. *Barriers to Proclaiming Freedom*
   Consider the emotional or social costs of publicly addressing injustice (pushback from family, fear of conflict, lack of institutional support). How does the Spirit empower you to overcome these barriers?

5. *Reimagining Church*
   If your congregation took Luke 4:18–19 as its primary blueprint, what would change in worship, outreach, or community engagement? How might you encourage such a shift?

Conclusion

When Jesus stood in the synagogue and proclaimed, "The Spirit of the Lord is upon me," He issued a transformative invitation for all who would follow Him. Far from being a polite, domesticated faith, Christianity—at its heart—is a radical movement fueled by the Holy Spirit, bent on healing the broken and restoring wholeness to individuals and societies. For Black women, whose histories bear the imprints of oppression, Luke

4:18–19 resonates as a clarion call to embrace our God-given gifts and voices for the sake of liberation.

In the midst of societal challenges like mass incarceration, healthcare inequities, and economic injustice, we are equipped by the Spirit to speak life, enact change, and walk alongside those who suffer. Through vibrant worship, anointing rituals, community initiatives, and freedom circles, we anchor our activism in God's power rather than our own limited resources. Each time we apply oil, lift our voices in prayer, or defend the marginalized, we echo Jesus' own mission—ensuring that His words continue to live among us: *"He has anointed me to bring good news to the poor... to proclaim release to the captives... to let the oppressed go free."*

May this Spirit-filled mandate inspire you to discover your unique role in furthering God's liberating reign. With the Holy Spirit anointing your efforts, you can rest in the assurance that you do not labor alone. As we each take up Jesus' mission, we do so in a holy collaboration—Black women, the broader church, and the world—journeying together toward freedom, hope, and the radiant reality of God's kingdom made manifest on earth.

Chapter 6

"Take Heart; I Have Overcome the World" (John 16:33)

"I have said this to you, so that in me you may have peace. In the world you face persecution. But take courage; I have conquered the world!"
—John 16:33 (NRSV)

When Jesus uttered the words "take courage; I have conquered the world" (NRSV) or "take heart; I have overcome the world" in John 16:33, He was preparing His disciples for the tribulations and conflicts they would soon encounter. Far from promising a life free of hardship, Jesus reassured them that His victory over sin and evil would sustain them through every trial. For Black women today, these words still resonate deeply. While we contend with racism, sexism, and socio-economic struggles, Christ's assurance reminds us that we need not battle alone. His overcoming presence empowers us to stand firm in faith, even when the odds seem stacked against us.

This chapter explores the context of Jesus' statement and connects it to contemporary challenges—particularly those faced by Black women. We will draw from liberation theology and womanist perspectives to reframe hardship as an opportunity for divine intervention. We will also examine practical strategies for building resilience—through counseling, community, and worship—and share real-life examples of Black women who have emerged victorious, testifying to God's sustaining power. Finally, we will offer reflection questions and action steps to help readers identify where they need to trust God for breakthrough and how to foster supportive networks that keep hope alive.

Context of Overcoming

Jesus' Words in a Time of Trial

The Gospel of John situates Jesus' promise of victory during His final discourse with His disciples (John 13–17). Aware of His impending arrest and crucifixion, Jesus provides comfort and instruction, forewarning His followers about coming trials. He paints a realistic portrait of persecution and sorrow, yet ends on a note of triumphant assurance: *"Take courage; I have conquered the world!"* (John 16:33).

For the early disciples, this meant they could face hostility, exile, and even martyrdom without being ultimately undone. In the midst of betrayal and violence, Jesus' victory—rooted in His divine nature and forthcoming resurrection—would anchor their faith. The promise extended beyond personal survival: it encompassed the mission of the nascent church, which would grow despite (and often because of) external pressures.

Modern Trials for Black Women

While modern Black women may not endure the exact kind of persecution that the first disciples faced, we confront our own set of tribulations. From persistent racial disparities in employment, healthcare, and education to the microaggressions and sexism that color daily interactions, these challenges can feel unrelenting. Socio-economic hurdles—such as wage gaps and gentrification—further intensify the struggle.

In faith communities, Black women may also face resistance or tokenism, especially in circles where leadership is still male-dominated. Yet Jesus' promise in John 16:33 offers hope amid these realities. His words remind us that even structural inequities do not have the final say. If Christ has already conquered the powers of evil, then the systems aligned with oppression are ultimately doomed. Our part is to stand in faith, work for justice, and believe that divine strength undergirds our every effort toward liberation.

Faith Over Fear
Liberation Theology and Christ's Victory

Liberation theologians emphasize the corporate and systemic dimensions of salvation. When Jesus declares, "I have conquered the world," He speaks not only of an individual's personal struggles but also of humanity's collective chains—oppressive systems, unjust hierarchies, and exploitative economies. Christ's victory thus emboldens communities to resist and dismantle structures that perpetuate injustice.

For Black women, this perspective affirms that our fight against racism, sexism, and economic exploitation is not an isolated endeavor; it is tied to the broader work of God in history. Christ's triumph means we are not powerless, even when statistics or media narratives suggest otherwise. Rather, we are co-laborers with a God who sides with the oppressed, empowering us to confront deep-seated injustices in academia, politics, healthcare, and beyond.

A Womanist Approach to Hardship

Womanist Theology reframes hardship as a potential site of divine revelation. While suffering is never glorified, it is recognized that God often meets us most profoundly in places of struggle. In this tradition, the testimonies of enslaved Black women, domestic workers, and civil rights activists serve as living parables: though they walked through the valley of systemic oppression, they encountered God's sustaining grace in communal prayer, spiritual songs, and Holy Spirit-led actions.

This approach neither trivializes suffering nor romanticizes it. Instead, it locates God's presence amid life's grit and complexity. Hardship becomes a space for divine intervention—an opportunity for the oppressed to experience a deeper measure of God's love and power. From a womanist perspective, Christ's triumph ensures that no sorrow, no injustice, and no heartbreak is beyond redemption. The abiding truth is that Jesus has already overcome the forces of darkness; our role is to trust His leading, even if the path is fraught with difficulty.

Concrete Strategies for Overcoming

Mental and Emotional Health Resources

Counseling and Therapy: Despite stigmas that sometimes discourage seeking professional help, therapy can be transformative for Black women navigating racial trauma, gender bias, and familial pressures. A Christian counselor or culturally competent therapist can help unpack generational wounds and offer coping strategies rooted in biblical principles. This is not a sign of weak faith; rather, it's an act of self-stewardship, allowing professional support to walk alongside spiritual formation.

Support Groups: Small groups—either in church or local community centers—can provide a safe space to share experiences and learn from one another. In these settings, common struggles become catalysts for collective wisdom and encouragement. The early church model of gathering in homes, breaking bread, and praying together (Acts 2:46) can inspire modern faith communities to form bonds that foster healing.

Spiritual Direction: A trained spiritual director can help individuals discern God's voice in their everyday lives. Particularly during seasons of adversity, spiritual direction offers a structured environment to reflect on biblical truths, prayer practices, and life decisions. This guidance can be especially beneficial for those sensing a call to ministry or activism but struggling with self-doubt or systemic barriers.

Hope Through Worship, Music, and Communal Praise

For many Black women, the Black Church tradition offers a vibrant wellspring of resilience. Music, in particular, plays a crucial role: from Negro spirituals to contemporary gospel anthems, songs have historically lifted weary hearts and unified communities in the face of oppression. Worship invites the Spirit to permeate our circumstances, reminding us of a reality greater than our immediate challenges.

Congregational Singing: Whether in traditional hymns or modern praise choruses, collective worship binds believers together, reinforcing shared faith and hope.

Dance and Creative Expression: Dance ministries and spoken word performances allow for bodily worship, turning anguish into artful praise. These expressions can break emotional chains and set hearts ablaze with renewed vision.

Testimony Services: In many Black churches, testifying is woven into weekly gatherings—believers share personal stories of God's intervention, encouraging one another to persevere. Hearing how others have overcome can embolden us to keep going.

Testimonies of Victory

Overcoming Personal Obstacles
Wilma Rudolph's Triumph Over Disability

Though not typically labeled a "theologian," Olympic sprinter

Wilma Rudolph offers a powerful story of perseverance. Born prematurely and contracting polio at a young age, Rudolph wore leg braces for much of her childhood. Yet through determination and faith in God, she eventually became the first American woman to win three gold medals in track and field during a single Olympic Games (1960). Her mother credited prayer and community support for Wilma's miraculous recovery. While she faced racism and segregation in her hometown, Rudolph's triumph became a beacon of hope, reflecting the principle that in Christ, our limitations don't define us—our faith and resolve do.

Shirley Caesar's Musical Journey

Renowned gospel singer **Pastor Shirley Caesar** grew up in poverty but clung to her faith. Starting her career in a small singing group, she later performed with the Caravans, one of the most influential gospel quartets, before launching a successful solo ministry. Despite setbacks and industry challenges, Caesar's unwavering trust in God fueled her longevity in gospel music and pastoral leadership. Her testimony underscores that even in a competitive and sometimes exploitative music industry, faith can anchor our gifts, leading to a ministry that spans decades.

Confronting Systemic Injustices

The "Mothers of the Movement"

In recent years, the mothers of Black men and women killed by police or vigilantes—like Sybrina Fulton (Trayvon Martin's mother) or Gwen Carr (Eric Garner's mother)—have mobilized for justice, using their grief as a clarion call for policy change. Though these women have faced unimaginable loss, many testify that their faith in God helps them endure. They have moved from personal tragedy to public advocacy, lobbying legislators and raising national awareness about police brutality. Their resilience illustrates how Christ's overcoming power can transform mourning into momentum for social reform.

Black Women in Academia and Advocacy
From Dr. Kimberlé Crenshaw (critical race theorist) to Dr. Melissa Harris-Perry (political scientist and commentator), numerous Black women in academic and public spheres confront systemic biases daily. Some, like Dr. Yolanda Pierce (Dean of Howard University School of Divinity), fuse scholarship with ministry, advocating for a more inclusive and justice-oriented theology. Their stories testify that God's victory extends to intellectual arenas, where dismantling racism, sexism, and homophobia often involves scholarly discourse, teaching, and policy-making.

Through these testimonies—both personal and systemic—we see a common thread: in each situation, faith in Christ's promise of victory propels Black women beyond despair. While the details differ, the underlying truth remains the same: Jesus' assurance that He has overcome the world emboldens us to face daunting odds, secure in the knowledge that we do not labor in vain.

Action Steps

Community Building: Form an accountability group or prayer circle that meets regularly to share burdens, celebrate victories, and strategize about social initiatives. Knowing you have a committed support system can provide renewed courage.

Advocacy Projects: Choose a local issue—like educational equity or prison reform—and develop a concrete plan to address it. This might include petitions, volunteer programs, or fundraising events tied to your church or neighborhood.

Mental Health Check-Ins: Encourage each group member to schedule at least one counseling session or pastoral care visit during high-stress seasons. Make it a group norm to discuss mental and emotional well-being openly.

Worship and Arts Night: Organize a special service or gathering that centers on music, poetry, and testimony related to overcoming adversity. Invite members to share personal stories of God's faithfulness. This can inspire deeper unity and remind everyone that they're part of a larger story of redemption.

Reflective Questions and Journal Prompts

1. *Naming Your Trials*

   Jesus speaks these words amid warnings of hardship. What specific trials—personal, familial, or systemic—feel most daunting to you right now? How does Christ's victory speak into those difficulties?

2. *Faith vs. Despair*

   In the face of unchanging realities like persistent racism or economic instability, how do you guard against despair? Which faith practices (worship, scriptural meditation, communal support) bolster your hope?

3. *Redefining 'Overcoming'*

   Does "overcoming the world" mean escaping hardship or finding strength to endure and transform it? How might a womanist perspective expand your understanding of what overcoming looks like?

4. *Testimonies of Triumph*

   Think of a Black woman you admire (friend, historical figure) who overcame immense obstacles. Which spiritual principles or communal factors contributed to her resilience?

5. *Community Resilience*

   What role do collective worship, music, and storytelling play in helping entire communities overcome systemic challenges? Can you envision a new tradition or gathering in your church or neighborhood that fosters corporate encouragement?

Conclusion

In John 16:33, Jesus does not sugarcoat the realities of life, especially for those who stand against societal ills or face personal hardships. Instead, He acknowledges the pain while offering a redemptive perspective: *Take heart; I have overcome the world.* This promise transcends time and place, resonating powerfully in the struggles of Black women who wrestle with racism, sexism, and socio-economic barriers. Liberation Theology and Womanist Theology together affirm that Christ's victory is not merely a future hope but a present source of resilience, fueling our faith in justice and wholeness.

As we embrace concrete strategies for emotional health, communal worship, and social advocacy, we embody Jesus' words in tangible ways—becoming conduits of healing and transformation. The testimonies of women who have risen above adversity underscore that the same Spirit who empowered Christ now empowers us to stand firm, serve others, and work toward a more just society. May these reflections and action steps encourage you to anchor your life in Christ's conquering love, carrying the conviction that no challenge—no matter how insurmountable it may appear—can overshadow the power of the One who has already overcome the world.

Chapter 7

"Ask and It Will Be Given to You; Seek and You Will Find" (Matthew 7:7)

"Ask, and it will be given you; search, and you will find; knock, and the door will be opened for you."
—Matthew 7:7 (NRSV)

In the Sermon on the Mount, Jesus issues an invitation that echoes the theme of *shameless audacity*: "Ask, and it will be given you; search, and you will find; knock, and the door will be opened for you." At first glance, this promise might seem almost too good to be true—especially for Black women who have often asked for fairness, opportunity, or justice only to encounter systemic barriers and disappointments. But rather than offering a superficial guarantee, Jesus calls us into a dynamic relationship with God, urging us to approach divine grace persistently and expectantly. In this chapter, we will explore how persistent prayer becomes a transformative force, fueling hope, resistance, and social action. Through historical examples and practical disciplines, we'll see how prayer is both a personal lifeline and a catalyst for communal change.

Power of Persistent Prayer

Revisiting the Theme of Shameless Audacity
Earlier in this book, we introduced the concept of *shameless audacity* from Luke 11, where a friend knocks at midnight until

he receives help. That same spirit resonates in Jesus' words in Matthew 7:7. The invitation to *ask, seek, and knock underscores* the proactive posture God calls us to adopt. Rather than retreating in the face of injustice or personal obstacles, we are to approach God boldly, confident that divine resources stand ready.

For Black women—navigating racial bias, gender discrimination, and socio-economic hurdles—this shameless audacity in prayer offers both solace and empowerment. It means refusing to believe that closed doors stay closed forever. It involves petitioning God with the raw honesty of someone who knows their survival might depend on the next breakthrough. From paying rent to advocating for policy reform, every need and dream can be brought before God, trusting that our voices matter in the heavenly courtroom.

Prayer as Resistance, Fueling Determination and Hope
In oppressive contexts, prayer can be an act of holy defiance. Throughout history, colonizers and slaveholders sought to limit or control Black religious expression, recognizing its power to foster unity and hope. Yet Black people prayed in hush harbors and secluded spaces, meeting in secret to call upon the same God who delivered the Israelites from Egypt. This clandestine prayer life subverted the narrative that enslaved people had no agency, reminding them of a higher authority who heard their cries.

That legacy continues. Persistent prayer confronts despair and cynicism, forces that can paralyze entire communities. Each time we bend the knee or lift our hands, we declare that our struggles are not the final word. We may wrestle with doubt or frustration, but in prayer we press forward—believing that God's justice will eventually break through the world's hardened systems. Like the friend at midnight, we knock, not in timid uncertainty, but in faith that the One behind the door is both loving and just.

Prayer as Protest and Prophecy

The History of Prayer in Black Church Traditions
Prayer meetings have long been the backbone of Black religious life. In many churches, the Wednesday night prayer service is as sacred as Sunday morning worship. Historically, these gatherings served more than just spiritual comfort; they became epicenters of social organization. Church mothers, often the chief intercessors, guided these gatherings with fervent pleas for God's intervention in personal and communal affairs.

During the civil rights era, activists like Dr. Martin Luther King Jr. and Fannie Lou Hamer invoked prayer openly, blending spiritual petition with social protest. For Hamer, prayer was the wellspring that fueled her work demanding voting rights for Black citizens. In her speeches, she often spontaneously broke into prayer or gospel hymns, transforming political rallies into spaces where God's presence was palpably invoked. This tradition endures today: whether in a church basement or on a virtual Zoom call, Black women lead prayer sessions that keep communities focused on both spiritual growth and tangible activism.

Undermining Systemic Evil by Keeping Hope Alive
It's no coincidence that oppressive powers seek to extinguish hope. When people lose hope, they become less likely to resist injustice. Persistent prayer subverts that hopelessness, connecting believers to a divine source that transcends earthly constraints. In her Pulitzer Prize–winning book *The Warmth of Other Suns*, Isabel Wilkerson recounts how many African Americans who left the South during the Great Migration leaned on prayer, trusting that God would guide them to better opportunities. This was not wishful thinking; it was a prophetic stance, anticipating a future shaped by God's redemptive power rather than the crushing weight of racism.

By praying for social justice—for example, against police brutality or inequitable schooling—Black women prophetically declare that the status quo is not God's final plan. Though it may take years or even generations, persistent prayer keeps the vision alive, emboldening activists, parents, pastors, and community organizers to keep pressing for change.

Practical Prayer Disciplines

Daily Devotion and Prayer Journals
Cultivating a prayer habit can transform everyday routines into sacred rhythms. Daily devotion might involve reading a short

passage of Scripture, meditating on its meaning, and then offering a brief prayer of thanksgiving or petition. Though simple, these moments of intentional connection with God recalibrate our perspective, reminding us whose we are.

Prayer journals serve as a written record of our dialogues with God. Writing prayers can deepen honesty—there's something about writing things down that encourages vulnerable confession and heartfelt praise. Over time, revisiting older entries helps us trace God's faithfulness, noticing where prayers have been answered, where lessons have been learned, and where hopes remain.

Corporate and Contemplative Prayer Styles

Corporate Prayer: Gathering with others (in-person or online) for focused prayer unites faith energies. Whether at weekly church intercession services or in smaller circles of trusted friends, corporate prayer amplifies the cry for justice and healing. One person's testimony can spark another's confidence, creating a synergy that propels an entire group forward.

Contemplative Prayer: Sometimes overshadowed in more charismatic settings, contemplative prayer is a powerful practice for slowing down and listening. Techniques like centering prayer or lectio divina (divine reading) encourage stillness, inviting the Holy Spirit to speak in the silence. Such practices can ground Black women who face relentless societal demands, offering a calming space to rest in God's presence and discern next steps for action.

Intercessory Prayer for Social Justice
Some issues weigh so heavily that they demand dedicated intercession.

Structured Prayer Guides: Creating a weekly or monthly guide that highlights specific justice concerns—police reform, healthcare access, affordable housing—and offers scriptural anchors to inform our prayers.

Focused Prayer Chains or Vigils: In the aftermath of a high-profile injustice, church groups can organize round-the-clock prayer chains, ensuring continuous corporate intercession. This collective focus both unites and energizes participants to explore additional ways to respond.

Public Prayer Walks: Some congregations and activists hold prayer walks through neighborhoods impacted by violence or neglect. By praying on-site, they bear witness to God's presence in areas often deemed hopeless, fostering relationships with residents and sparking communal renewal.

Womanist Perspective on Asking and Seeking

Fostering Spiritual Intimacy and Social Awareness
Womanist Theology contends that prayer must never be divorced from lived experience. In the wake of trauma or

systemic oppression, prayer becomes a vehicle for expressing lament, but also for cultivating resilience. Black women's prayers often encompass a broad spectrum of emotions—anger, sorrow, joy, gratitude—reflecting a refusal to censor our full humanity before God.

This openness fosters a deeper intimacy with the Divine. When we cry out for deliverance from a rigged system, we align with the biblical psalmists who lamented injustice yet clung to God's steadfast love. When we rejoice in small victories—like a scholarship awarded or a community center opening—we affirm that God is at work in the details of our lives. Through these cycles of lament and praise, prayer shapes our hearts to love what God loves, heightening our awareness of societal ills and urging us to act.

Discernment: Recognizing God's Answers and Open Doors

Asking and seeking imply readiness to receive or find. Yet we sometimes overlook God's answers because they don't arrive in the form we expect. A job opportunity may fall through, only for another door to open that better aligns with our calling. We might pray for patience and find ourselves facing situations that test our resolve, thereby *developing* the very character we asked God to cultivate. Discernment is key.

From a womanist lens, discernment includes reflecting on communal wisdom. Talking with elders, prayer partners, or mentors can shed light on how God might be moving. We learn to sense the Holy Spirit's nudges in everyday life—whether through a timely conversation, a confirming Scripture passage, or an unexpected shift in circumstances. By staying alert, we honor Jesus' invitation not only to ask and seek but also to *notice* when our requests are answered in unforeseen ways.

Action-Based Faith

Prayer and Praxis Working Hand in Hand

Biblical faith is never merely theoretical; it's meant to bear fruit in action. James 2:17 (NRSV) reminds us that "faith by itself, if it has no works, is dead." This truth resonates with Jesus' words to ask and seek: we cannot simply request God's intervention while refusing to participate in the solutions God provides. Real prayer propels us into engagement.

Advocating for Policy Change: Praying for an end to police brutality should accompany real steps—voting for reform-minded candidates, lobbying for legislation, or joining a local police accountability board.

Developing Community Initiatives: If we pray about educational disparities, we can also volunteer as tutors, serve on the PTA, or fundraise for scholarships.

Supporting Mental Health: If interceding for those battling depression or anxiety, consider supporting mental health programs, sharing resources, or offering transportation to therapy sessions.

When prayer leads us to roll up our sleeves and get involved, we begin to see how God often answers prayers *through* our availability and obedience.

Women's Ministries and Outreach Programs Birthed in Prayer
Many transformative ministries have humble origins in prayer circles.

Missionary Societies in the Black Church, historically led by women, which started as small groups praying for overseas missions but eventually expanded to address local poverty and literacy.

Mothers' Boards and **Women's Auxiliaries**, where older church mothers mentor younger women. Such boards frequently shape church policy behind the scenes, supporting pastors with prayer and offering practical solutions for congregational needs.

Grassroots Non-Profits like *Mothers of the Movement* are born from grief and sustained by fervent prayer as they seek policy reforms. Some women have launched counseling centers or after-school programs because they sensed a divine call to fill a community gap.

In each case, prayer acted as the seed, faith as the water, and God's Spirit as the sunshine—bringing forth ministries that now serve hundreds or thousands of people.

Reflective Questions and Journal Prompts

1. *Hesitations in Asking*

   Many of us hesitate to ask God (or others) for help, fearing rejection or disappointment. Reflect on a time you held back from making a request. How might stepping out in "shameless audacity" have changed the outcome?

2. *Persistence vs. Entitlement*

   How do you distinguish between bold, faith-filled persistence and a sense of entitlement? Where does humility fit into your approach to prayer and seeking?

3. *Prayer as Resistance*

   In historically oppressed communities, prayer has often doubled as protest—fueling hope and collective action. How can your prayers today energize social justice work rather than remaining a private exercise?

4. *Listening for Answers*

   Jesus promises that those who knock will find an open door. Have you experienced answers to prayer that looked different than you expected? What helps you stay attentive to God's creative responses?

5. *Turning Prayer into Praxis*

Identify one social issue (e.g., healthcare inequality, environmental racism) that weighs on your heart. In addition to praying, what concrete step could you take this week to address that issue?

Conclusion

Jesus' invitation to "ask, and it will be given you; search, and you will find" is neither a trite formula nor a path to instant gratification. Rather, it's an invitation into a living conversation with God, one that empowers and emboldens us to confront life's hardships with shameless audacity. For Black women, prayer has been and continues to be a life-giving force: it fuels resistance against systemic oppression, comforts us in personal crises, and aligns our hearts with God's vision for justice and wholeness.

Through persistent prayer, we remember that no door is truly beyond the reach of heaven's keys. While the timetable may challenge our patience, and the answers may not always resemble our initial expectations, faith-filled petition keeps hope alive in our communities. As you integrate the prayer practices and womanist perspectives discussed in this chapter, trust that every knock on heaven's door resounds in the presence of a God who hears and cares. And when you arise from prayer, step forward with confidence into the opportunities God provides, knowing that ask-seek-knock is the heartbeat of a vibrant, transformative faith—one that leaves an indelible mark on the world around us.

Chapter 8

"Whoever Wants to Be My Disciple Must Deny Themselves" (Luke 9:23)

"Then he said to them all, 'If any want to become my followers, let them deny themselves and take up their cross daily and follow me.'"
—Luke 9:23 (NRSV)

Jesus' words in Luke 9:23 have often been quoted to emphasize the cost of discipleship: *"If any want to become my followers, let them deny themselves and take up their cross daily and follow me."* Yet the phrase "deny themselves" can be easily misunderstood—especially in contexts where Black women have historically been expected to suppress their own well-being for the benefit of others. In this chapter, we will explore the biblical call to self-denial and distinguish it from oppressive forms of self-negation. We will then delve into how womanist theology offers a corrective, reclaiming Christ's invitation as a pathway to liberated service rather than a demand for silence or self-erasure. Finally, we will outline practical disciplines and reflective practices that help us strike a healthy balance between sacrificial love and self-care.

Discipleship and Self-Denial

Clarifying the Difference Between Oppressive Self-Negation and Biblical Self-Denial

In many Christian traditions, denying oneself is equated with humility, obedience, and surrender to God's will. *Biblical* self-denial, however, does not mean hating oneself or denying one's own humanity. Instead, it is a posture of prioritizing God's desires above personal ego or ambition. When Jesus calls us to "deny ourselves," He is challenging us to abandon the illusions of self-sufficiency, pride, or rigid control over our lives. This is not about diminishing our personhood; it is about recognizing that the deepest fulfillment comes from aligning our will with God's.

In contrast, *oppressive self-negation* arises when a community or institution coerces individuals—often women or marginalized groups—to give without boundaries or to stifle their own growth, voice, or identity. For Black women, this can take the form of constant labor without rest, serving as the family's or church's "workhorse," or being told to "just pray about it" rather than addressing legitimate emotional and physical needs. Such distortions misuse Scripture to perpetuate burnout and silence, rather than fostering a dynamic, life-giving relationship with God.

Potential Conflicts with Self-Care and Healthy Boundaries

Christ's invitation to self-denial can appear to clash with modern discussions about self-care. After all, are we not called to love our neighbors as ourselves (Mark 12:31)? Doesn't that verse imply we must *value* ourselves appropriately to extend genuine care to others?

The tension lies in interpreting what "deny yourselves" means in practical terms. A biblical framework recognizes that our bodies and minds are temples of the Holy Spirit (1 Corinthians 6:19). Honoring God involves stewardship of these temples, which includes rest, nourishment, and emotional well-being. True discipleship transforms selfish desires into selfless love, but it never negates the God-given worth of the individual. When self-denial is rightly understood, it leads to *holy generosity*—not self-destruction.

Womanist Caution

Recognizing Misuse of "Deny Yourself" Against Black Women

Womanist theologians have long pointed out how scriptures calling for submission or self-sacrifice can be weaponized against Black women. Historically, the church sometimes preached that Black women should "deny themselves" to the point of silent suffering—whether enduring abusive relationships, exploitative labor, or mental health crises without relief. Some were told they lacked faith if they sought rest or questioned patriarchal leadership.

This misuse of Scripture ignores the larger gospel narrative, where Jesus actively restores dignity and agency to marginalized people—like the woman bent over for eighteen years (Luke 13:10–13) or the Samaritan woman at the well (John 4:7–42). Far from erasing them, Jesus listens to their stories, affirms their worth, and empowers them to speak. When we apply Jesus' command out of context, we risk perpetuating systems of harm rather than embodying the wholeness Christ intended.

A Corrective: Authentic Discipleship vs. Silence and Self-Erasure

Authentic discipleship compels believers to sacrifice their *ego*, not their fundamental identity. For Black women, this means following Christ without abandoning our cultural roots, spiritual gifts, or mental health. It also means resisting the lie that we must shrink ourselves to appease others.

Womanist theologians underscore that Christ's call involves mutuality, communal uplift, and a solidarity that resists individualism but not individuality. Yes, we lay down pride, but we do not silence the voice God has given us. Yes, we relinquish self-importance, but we do not discard our rightful place at God's table. In short, self-denial is not about being voiceless; it's about being *Christ-centered*. This shift liberates Black women to serve with joy and purpose, rather than from obligation or guilt.

Reframing Sacrifice

Letting Go of Ego, Pride, and the World's Definition of Success

Jesus' command in Luke 9:23 calls us to lay aside superficial measures of achievement—whether that's societal status, material wealth, or constant self-promotion. Instead, we are invited to root our worth in God's love and plan. Sacrifice, then, becomes an act of freedom: we detach from worldly accolades so we can pursue divine approval, which is inherently more satisfying and eternal in scope.

Ego: The desire for recognition or power can overshadow God's leading. Denying ourselves means acknowledging God's sovereignty—"Lord, You increase; I decrease" (cf. John 3:30).

Pride: Pride disguises itself as self-righteousness or entitlement. Christ-like humility acknowledges that everything we have—gifts, opportunities, resources—ultimately comes from God.

Earthly Success: The world's yardstick might measure success in titles, possessions, or social media clout. Kingdom success, however, is marked by love, justice, mercy, and faithfulness (Micah 6:8).

Scriptural Examples of Women Retaining Agency in Following Christ

Mary Magdalene: She is often remembered for her devoted witness to Jesus' resurrection (John 20:11–18). Although she faced societal stigmas, she did not lose her sense of self in discipleship; rather, she gained a renewed identity as a herald of the gospel. Her encounter with the risen Christ empowered her to speak boldly to the male apostles—a move that would have been culturally transgressive.

Mary, the Mother of Jesus: The ultimate example of self-denial rooted in faith, Mary consents to bear the Messiah in Luke 1:38, saying, "Here am I, the servant of the Lord; let it be with me according to your word." Yet her humility does not erase her agency. At the wedding in Cana (John 2), Mary confidently advocates for a miracle, nudging Jesus into public ministry. She embodies both submission to God's will and an assertive maternal role, demonstrating that self-denial is compatible with God-given assertiveness and leadership.

These examples show that denying oneself in Scripture is far from passive. It involves relinquishing control to God while actively participating in the divine mission. The result is not diminished women but *empowered* disciples.

Concrete Practices of Discipleship

Service Projects, Church, and Community Roles
Local Outreach: Participate in or organize projects that address community needs, like food drives, tutoring programs, or health fairs. Service humbles us by shifting the focus from our own desires to the pressing concerns of neighbors and strangers alike.

Church Ministries: From leading worship to mentoring youth, church roles offer a structured way to exercise spiritual gifts. Authentic self-denial within these ministries recognizes that the end goal is to exalt Christ and bless the community, not to accrue personal prestige.

Mentorship of Younger Women: Older generations are encouraged to guide younger women in faith and life (Titus 2:3–5). For Black women, mentorship can break cycles of poverty, low self-esteem, or lack of academic opportunity. Denying ourselves to invest in younger sisters fosters a culture of generational uplift rather than competition.

Spiritual Habits Aligned with Jesus' Heart

Fasting: By abstaining from meals or certain comforts, we temporarily forego physical gratification, creating space to focus on God's priorities. Whether a half-day or a week-long fast, the goal is not to punish the body but to gain spiritual clarity and intimacy with God.

Almsgiving: Generosity is a hallmark of discipleship. Whether donating finances, clothing, or time, almsgiving reminds us that we steward resources on God's behalf. This act of self-denial challenges materialism and cultivates empathy for those who are economically vulnerable.

Volunteering: Sacrificing leisure time to serve consistently in a local shelter, elderly home, or youth center hones self-discipline. Volunteering also expands our worldview, revealing systemic inequities and deepening compassion, both of which reflect the heart of Jesus.

Balancing Self-Care and Service

Ensuring "Denying Self" Doesn't Become Self-Destructive

Black women already carry significant societal burdens; thus, we must discern carefully between life-giving sacrifice and detrimental overextension. Spiritual maturity involves identifying when God calls us to *rest* rather than to "push through." Overwork and chronic stress do not glorify God; they undermine the abundant life Jesus promises (John 10:10).

Some practical safeguards include:

Regular Check-Ins: Ask trusted friends or a pastor to help you evaluate your emotional, physical, and spiritual health.

Sabbath Rhythm: Dedicate one day a week, or at least a portion of a day, to rest and spiritual rejuvenation, mirroring God's own pattern (Genesis 2:2–3).

Therapy or Spiritual Direction: Engaging with a professional or trained guide can unearth hidden patterns of self-neglect masked as "service."

Jesus' Example of Prayer and Rest

Throughout the Gospels, Jesus models balance. He heals crowds, feeds thousands, and relentlessly teaches—but He also retreats to solitary places to pray (Luke 5:16). After intense seasons of ministry, He withdraws with His disciples for reflection and rest (Mark 6:31). If the Son of God needed moments of pause, how much more do we?

When practicing self-denial, we can look to Jesus' pattern of: *Rising Early to Pray (Mark 1:35):* Before the hustle of the day began, Jesus sought renewal in the Father's presence.

Setting Boundaries (Mark 3:9): Jesus sometimes told the crowds He needed space, getting into a boat to teach or cross the lake.

Accepting Help (Luke 8:1–3): Women like Mary Magdalene, Joanna, and Susanna supported Jesus' ministry financially and practically. Even Christ did not refuse assistance, underscoring that humble dependence is not contrary to self-denial.

Reflective Questions and Journal Prompts

1. *Understanding Self-Denial*
   What does "deny yourself" mean in your context? How do you differentiate healthy self-denial (releasing ego, pride) from harmful self-negation (silencing your worth, ignoring your needs)?

2. *Breaking Misconceptions*

   Reflect on any past teachings that used "deny yourself" to justify exploiting Black women's labor or emotional capacity. How can you reframe this verse in a way that honors your dignity?

3. *Following Jesus' Model*

   Jesus often withdrew to pray, showed compassion, and also held people accountable. How does His example expand your view of self-denial?

4. *Identifying Ego Attachments*

   Which aspects of cultural success—status, social media acclaim, material gain—do you cling to? What steps might help you relinquish those attachments and live more fully for God?

5. *Serving with Joy*

   In what areas can you serve your church or community without feeling coerced or depleted? Share one commitment you'll make this month to practice life-giving discipleship that respects both self-care and the needs of others.

Conclusion

Luke 9:23's directive—"If any want to become my followers, let them deny themselves"—beckons us into the heart of discipleship: a life oriented around God rather than self. Rightly understood, this call leads to freedom, not bondage. It requires relinquishing ego, pride, and worldly definitions of success, while retaining the God-given dignity that empowers us to serve joyfully. For Black women, the womanist critique is essential, cautioning us against toxic forms of self-denial that have been historically misapplied to justify exploitation or silence.

Authentic biblical sacrifice does not erase our voices or deplete our identities; it allows Christ's love to saturate every aspect of our being. Through concrete practices—service, spiritual disciplines, and intentional rest—we learn to balance our call to selfless ministry with the care of our own bodies, minds, and souls. Ultimately, we follow a Savior who not only laid down His life but also rose again, showing that true denial of self opens the way to transformation, resurrection, and the abundant life God desires for all.

Chapter 9
"I Am the Good Shepherd" (John 10:11)

"I am the good shepherd. The good shepherd lays down his life for the sheep."
—John 10:11 (NRSV)

In John 10:11, Jesus identifies Himself as the "good shepherd," evoking a pastoral image that resonates across centuries. For ancient communities, shepherding was a labor-intensive and deeply relational occupation, requiring constant vigilance, protection, and care for a flock. Today, as Black women navigate the complexities of modern life—racism, sexism, socio-economic barriers, and family responsibilities—Jesus' self-revelation as a shepherd offers comfort and assurance that we are neither invisible nor unprotected. This chapter examines the scriptural roots of shepherd imagery and reflects on how a womanist understanding of God's nurturing character speaks to the lived realities of Black women. We will explore practical ways to lean on the Good Shepherd's guidance and highlight stories of care and protection that demonstrate God's faithfulness in unexpected ways.

Shepherd Imagery in Scripture
Role of Shepherds in Biblical Times
Shepherding in the ancient Near East was no easy task. Shepherds were responsible for leading sheep to water and

pasture, guarding them from predators, and tending to their wounds. Unlike modern-day ranchers who might manage livestock from a distance, biblical shepherds stayed intimately close to their flocks, often living outdoors with them and calling them by name. This close proximity created a bond of trust: the sheep followed the shepherd's voice because they recognized it as the source of protection and provision.

This culturally rich backdrop helps us appreciate the depth of Jesus' words. When He declares, "I am the good shepherd," He is not merely employing a pretty metaphor. He's asserting a profound commitment to those who belong to Him—a commitment so strong that He would lay down His life for His sheep. This promise stands at the heart of the Christian gospel, underscoring divine love manifested in sacrificial leadership.

Comfort and Assurance in Jesus' Shepherd Role
Throughout Scripture, shepherd imagery signals care, guidance, and covenant faithfulness. Psalm 23, perhaps the most famous shepherd passage, poetically depicts God as a provider and protector who leads us beside still waters and restores our souls. Similarly, Jesus' statement in John 10:11 echoes the tenderness of that Old Testament tradition, yet with a critical New Testament perspective: the shepherd does not merely guide but willingly sacrifices Himself for the flock.

For Black women, this shepherd imagery can be especially comforting in times of uncertainty or adversity. Whether dealing with workplace discrimination, financial strain, or exhaustion from caregiving roles, knowing that Jesus stands as a protective and attentive figure can embolden us to keep moving forward. His words imply that we are deeply known, cherished, and safe under divine watch.

Womanist Vision of Divine Care

Emphasizing God's Nurturing Dimension

Womanist Theology uplifts the nurturing, life-giving aspects of God, often drawing parallels to maternal figures and communal bonds among Black women. Historically, Black communities have relied on "church mothers" and matriarchs who provided not just physical sustenance—cooking meals, nursing wounds—but also spiritual counsel and emotional support. These women functioned much like shepherds, guiding younger generations through perilous social and cultural terrains.

When Jesus calls Himself the "good shepherd," we can see echoes of these motherly qualities: watchfulness, compassion, and willingness to intervene for the vulnerable. This vision counters stereotypes that frame God as distant or exclusively authoritarian. Instead, we encounter a God who is intimately invested in our well-being, gently leading us toward growth, justice, and rest.

The Good Shepherd for Marginalized Communities

Marginalized communities, including Black women, often battle systemic injustice and a sense of invisibility in broader society.

But in God's economy, the "least of these" receive special attention. The Good Shepherd parable (Luke 15:3–7) pictures a shepherd leaving ninety-nine sheep in safety to seek out one that is lost or endangered—a radical image of love that prioritizes the vulnerable. This aspect of God's character resonates deeply with those on society's margins.

For Black women, understanding God as a shepherd who actively seeks out and protects can validate our experiences of being overlooked or oppressed. We are not just stray sheep left to navigate rough terrains alone. Rather, the Good Shepherd is attuned to our struggles—ready to step into hostile environments and lead us to spaces of healing, rest, and affirmation.

Dependence on Divine Guidance

Trusting God's Voice Amid Conflicting Cultural Messages

In a world saturated with conflicting advice—media influencers, political figures, corporate ads—it can be challenging to discern which voices genuinely align with God's best for us. Black women, in particular, may receive messages that question our competence, belittle our achievements, or feed us stereotypes about "strong Black womanhood" that leave no room for vulnerability or rest.

Learning to trust the Good Shepherd involves cultivating an ear attuned to divine wisdom. Just as sheep learn to recognize their shepherd's voice, we develop spiritual discernment through consistent engagement with Scripture, prayer, and community. When cultural messages conflict with biblical values of justice, compassion, and humility, we can lean into God's guidance, believing that the shepherd's voice never leads to exploitation or harm.

Listening Prayer, Spiritual Discernment, and Wise Counsel

Listening Prayer: Setting aside time for silent reflection—free from the noise of technology and daily obligations—helps us become more sensitive to God's promptings. In these moments, we can offer our fears and questions, asking the Holy Spirit to clarify next steps.

Spiritual Discernment: This broader process involves weighing decisions or beliefs against Scripture, personal conviction, and communal accountability. For instance, if we sense a call to activism in our neighborhood, we might seek confirmation through prayer partners or trusted mentors who can help us see God's hand at work.

Wise Counsel: Scripture encourages us to seek "a multitude of counselors" (Proverbs 15:22). Whether it's church elders, mental health professionals, or knowledgeable peers, counsel from others can shed light on blind spots and confirm the leading of the Good Shepherd in our lives.

Practical Ways to Lean on the Good Shepherd

Engaging Scripture and Practicing Lectio Divina

A consistent study of Scripture, particularly passages highlighting God's faithfulness, fortifies trust in the Good Shepherd. **Lectio Divina** is an ancient practice of slow, meditative reading. Rather than consuming large chunks of text, you read a small passage multiple times, pausing to reflect on words or phrases that resonate. This contemplative method allows the Word to penetrate deeply, opening space for the Holy Spirit to speak personally about areas where you need guidance or reassurance.

Suggested Bible passages for Lectio Divina related to the Good Shepherd might include Psalm 23, Ezekiel 34 (where God critiques negligent shepherds and promises to shepherd the flock), and John 10:1–18. As you read, imagine yourself as one of the sheep in these stories—vulnerable but protected, uncertain but led by a benevolent guide.

Forming "Shepherd Circles" for Mutual Support

Communal support amplifies our experience of God's shepherding care. **Shepherd Circles** can be small groups of women—friends, church members, or coworkers—who gather regularly for prayer, accountability, and shared wisdom.

In these circles:

Scripture Study: Each meeting can begin with a short Bible passage on God's care or guidance, followed by open reflection.

Personal Check-Ins: Members share praises, struggles, and questions, receiving collective prayer and counsel.

Action Steps: Groups might choose a communal project—like supporting a single mother or volunteering at a homeless shelter—to express divine care tangibly.

By walking alongside one another, we collectively model the shepherd's heart, offering protection, encouragement, and guidance.

Stories of Care and Protection

God's shepherding often appears through ordinary events, unexpected encounters, or a series of divine "coincidences" that can't be chalked up to mere chance. Below are examples of how the Good Shepherd has guided and sheltered real people in their life journeys.

Overcoming Financial Hardship

Tamika's Tuition Miracle

Tamika, a single mother of two, felt called to return to college but feared crushing debt. While praying one morning, she sensed a nudge to apply for a scholarship program at a nearby university—one she'd previously overlooked. Two months later, she learned she'd been awarded full tuition and a stipend for childcare. Tamika credits this "miracle" to God's guidance, pointing out she had a quiet sense of peace when she submitted the application, despite the odds. The scholarship not only allowed her to complete her degree but also positioned her for a new career that aligned with her gifts.

Protection in Times of Danger
Angela's Unexpected Detour

Angela was driving home late one night from choir rehearsal when she felt an inexplicable urge to take a different route. Although she usually stuck to the main highway, she decided to follow the detour in her spirit. The next day, she learned that a serious accident occurred on her usual route around the same time she would have been passing through. Angela interprets her deviation as divine protection—proof that the Good Shepherd is attuned even to our daily commutes.

Emotional and Spiritual Healing
Gwen's Recovery from Church Hurt

After experiencing betrayal in her church community, Gwen struggled with anger and depression. She felt spiritually disoriented, as though she couldn't hear God's voice anymore. In desperation, she joined a small women's Bible study focused on God's promises of restoration. Over several months, she found healing through honest conversations and persistent prayer, gradually rediscovering a sense of belonging. Gwen says the Good Shepherd met her in her deepest pain, using fellow believers to guide her back into the fold with renewed faith.

Reflective Questions and Journal Prompts

1. *Experiencing Divine Shepherding*

   Consider a time you felt God's guidance or protection. How did that experience shape your trust in the "Good Shepherd"?

2. *Shepherding Others*

   We often think of ourselves as sheep, but sometimes God calls us to shepherd. In which spaces (home, church, community) are you called to guide, protect, or nurture others?

3. *Rest vs. Overwork*

   Shepherds lead sheep to rest in green pastures. Are you allowing yourself true rest, or are you perpetually in motion? Reflect on what "still waters" could look like in your life.

4. *Overcoming Distrust*

   If you've been hurt by church leaders or authority figures, how does Jesus' gentle shepherd image challenge your fears about leadership and pastoral care?

5. *Belonging to the Flock*

   Do you see yourself as part of a broader community under God's care? How can you deepen collective bonds, ensuring that no one in your circle feels lost or isolated?

Conclusion

Jesus' assurance, "I am the good shepherd," stands as a testament to God's intimate involvement in our daily lives. While modern challenges can sometimes obscure this truth, a womanist perspective on divine care underscores that no marginalization or hardship renders us invisible to the Shepherd's watchful eye. Our call is to listen for His voice amid societal clamor, trust in His guidance, and cooperate with His leading—even when it nudges us toward detours or deeper vulnerability.

By embracing practices like Lectio Divina, forming supportive circles, and sharing testimonies of divine intervention, we cultivate a communal and personal awareness of God's ongoing shepherding. In doing so, we not only receive comfort and direction ourselves but also become conduits of that same nurturing grace to others. May the Good Shepherd's presence sustain you as you journey forward, confident that the One who laid down His life for the sheep continues to guide, protect, and restore each of us in ways both seen and unseen.

Chapter 10

"I Have Come That They May Have Life...to the Full" (John 10:10)

"The thief comes only to steal and kill and destroy. I came that they may have life, and have it abundantly."
—John 10:10 (NRSV)

John 10:10 is among the most hopeful promises in Scripture: Jesus declares His purpose is to give life in all its fullness. In a world marked by exploitation, injustice, and dehumanizing narratives, this assurance stands as a beacon of hope, especially for Black women who endure the compounded weight of racial, gender, and economic inequalities. Rather than a superficial "prosperity" message, Jesus' words point to a holistic liberation—one that addresses spiritual, emotional, communal, and social needs.

This final chapter synthesizes the themes we have explored throughout this book, focusing on the promise of *abundant life* in Christ. We will clarify what Jesus means by "life to the full," examine its links to liberation theology and womanist flourishing, and offer practical suggestions for cultivating and celebrating this gift. Ultimately, abundant life is not merely an individual blessing; it extends to families, communities, and systems that reflect God's justice and joy.

Abundant Life Defined

What Does Jesus Mean by "Abundant Life"?

When Jesus says, "I came that they may have life, and have it abundantly," He envisions more than just physical survival. The Greek word for "life" here—*zōē*—emphasizes vitality, well-being, and wholeness. It encompasses:

- **Spiritual Wholeness**: An intimate relationship with God that brings inner peace and guides ethical living.

- **Justice and Community**: A collective flourishing where resources are shared equitably and society mirrors divine compassion.

- **Joy and Fulfillment**: The freedom to celebrate our God-given gifts, relationships, and achievements without fear or shame.

This definition inherently challenges scarcity mentalities—the belief that there's never enough time, love, or resources to go around. It also confronts oppressive structures that hoard benefits for the few at the expense of the many. Jesus' statement sets Him in direct opposition to all forces—both spiritual and societal—that "steal and kill and destroy" life.

Challenging Scarcity and Oppressive Systems

For Black women, "scarcity" can be an ever-present narrative: scarce job opportunities, scarce healthcare resources, scarce recognition for cultural contributions. Meanwhile, oppressive systems—racism, sexism, classism—further restrict avenues for flourishing. But Jesus' promise of abundant life stands as a critique of these inequities. It invites us to see beyond the limitations that society imposes, trusting that God's resources are sufficient to meet our needs and exceed our expectations.

When we adopt this perspective, we resist internalizing messages of unworthiness or lack. We begin to anticipate God's restorative power in personal, communal, and systemic arenas. Far from fueling complacency, the knowledge that God desires our flourishing motivates us to align ourselves with justice, generosity, and mutual uplift.

Liberation Theology's Fullness

The Broad Scope of Jesus' Mission
Liberation theology underscores that Jesus' mission was never narrowly spiritual. He didn't just forgive sins; He fed the hungry, healed the sick, and announced freedom to the oppressed (Luke 4:18–19). Abundant life, therefore, encompasses physical, emotional, social, and spiritual dimensions. It confronts structural injustices—like poverty or mass incarceration—while nurturing inner transformation and reconciliation.

For Black women who face cultural erasure and systemic violence, this holistic gospel message is profoundly relevant. It insists that God cares about affordable housing, wage equity, reproductive health, and safe neighborhoods just as much as personal piety. *All* of these factors shape how we experience abundant life.

Equity, Peace, and Flourishing for the Oppressed

In liberation theology, the phrase "preferential option for the poor" encapsulates God's special concern for the marginalized. When Jesus declares abundant life for His followers, He envisions a community where no one is left in desperation. For this reason, activism becomes a spiritual discipline: standing against unjust laws, advocating for policy changes, and redistributing resources align with Jesus' liberating mandate.

Black women have historically led such efforts, often without formal recognition. From Harriet Tubman's Underground Railroad to contemporary organizers fighting for voting rights, these trailblazers enact abundant life for themselves and future generations. Their work demonstrates that Jesus' promise isn't just for individuals but for societies yearning to reflect divine equity and compassion.

Womanist Flourishing

Joy and Creativity as Integral to Spiritual Life

Womanist theology highlights the importance of *delight* and *celebration*, reminding us that spiritual life isn't solely about endurance through suffering. Indeed, laughter, music, art, and dance offer powerful expressions of faith, especially in communities that have resisted oppression by cherishing communal joy. Whether through gospel choirs, soulful cooking, or vibrant church hats, Black women have long reclaimed spaces of happiness as a form of resistance and divine fellowship.

Joy coexists with sorrow. It does not negate the harsh realities we face but infuses them with hope. Embracing joy—as a conscious decision to honor God's goodness—becomes an act of spiritual warfare against despair. By celebrating our bodies, cultures, and achievements, we testify that the thief's attempts to destroy our dignity do not have the final say.

Cultural Wealth and Expressions of Abundant Life
The cultural wealth of Black women is vast: music that reverberates in sanctuaries and protest marches, storytelling traditions that preserve ancestral wisdom, and cuisine that fosters communal bonds. Each represents a dimension of abundant life, defying narrow definitions of success. Womanist flourishing includes nurturing relationships (with neighbors, church folks, and extended kin) and recognizing the holy in everyday moments—sitting around a kitchen table, braiding hair, or singing praises in a storefront church.

By honoring these creative and relational gifts, we resist assimilationist pressures that ignore or undermine our heritage. Instead, we model a holistic spirituality—one that finds God's presence in feasting and fellowship, in spirited dancing and communal lament, all woven together by a deep reverence for life.

Practical Applications

Cultivating Fullness through Holistic Health and Community

Physical Exercise and Rest: Incorporate movement into daily routines—walks, dance classes, or gentle stretching. Equally vital is adequate sleep, something Black women often sacrifice due to multiple demands. Honoring our bodies affirms that God cares about our wellness.

Mental Health Awareness: Seek therapy, counseling, or spiritual direction if stress, anxiety, or trauma hinder joy. Mental health is integral to abundant life, and professional support can offer coping strategies aligned with faith.

Life-Giving Relationships: Build circles of trust—friends who encourage, pastors who listen, neighbors who watch out for each other. These connections reflect God's design for us to flourish in community, not isolation.

Community Activism: Engage in local or national organizations dedicated to social justice, from voting rights to prison reform. By investing time and resources, we extend abundant life beyond personal boundaries.

Dream-Building and Collective Support

Vision Boards: Creating a collage of scriptures, quotes, and images that represent your God-inspired aspirations can serve as a visual reminder of the abundant life you're pursuing.

Prayerfully review it, asking God to open doors and refine your vision.

Goal Setting: Rather than drifting through life, discern how you can align your passions with kingdom values. Break down goals into actionable steps—whether it's starting a small business, returning to school, or launching a community program.

Collective Support Networks: Join or form groups (church-based or otherwise) where members hold each other accountable to goals and celebrate milestones. In these circles, success is shared, not hoarded, reflecting the mutual flourishing Jesus envisions.

Reflective Questions and Journal Prompts

1. *Defining Abundance*
   When you hear "life to the full," do you picture financial gain, emotional well-being, spiritual empowerment—or all of the above? How might Jesus' definition of abundance differ from consumer culture?

2. *Confronting Scarcity Mindsets*
   In what ways do systemic inequalities perpetuate the belief that there isn't enough to go around? How can faith in God's provision help overcome fears of scarcity?

3. *Cultural Expressions of Joy*
   Music, dance, storytelling, and fashion have long been part of Black women's creative resilience. Which cultural expressions most energize you and connect you to God's life-giving spirit?

4. *Dream-Building*

   Make a list of dreams you've put on hold or deemed "unrealistic."
   What steps of faith (vision boards, mentoring, journaling) could
   help you reclaim those dreams for God's glory?

5. *Inviting Others into Abundance*

   True abundance fosters communal uplift. How can you share your
   blessings—whether time, resources, or advocacy—so others
   experience the fullness God intends?

Final Reflection and Celebration

A Brief Litany of Thanksgiving
God of Abundance,

We thank You for the wide expanse of Your mercy and grace.

We thank You for creating us in Your image, for calling us Your
children.

We rejoice in every victory won and every milestone reached.

We ask for courage to build communities of justice and
solidarity.

We affirm our dignity, our gifts, and our capacity to dream big.

May we walk in the fullness of life that Jesus promised—

Bound together in hope, guided by love, sustained by faith.

Amen.

Celebrating Milestones and Victories
Part of abundant life is recognizing and commemorating
progress, however small. In a world that often highlights deficits
and failures, pausing to celebrate is a profoundly
countercultural act. Whether you're marking a personal

achievement (finishing a degree, paying off debt, overcoming a health challenge) or a community success (securing a grant, organizing a protest that led to reform), take time to rejoice in these blessings. Host a small gathering, share testimonies at church, or post words of gratitude on social media—whatever suits your personality and community context. By doing so, you proclaim that God's goodness is real and active in the present moment.

Conclusion

Jesus' declaration, "I came that they may have life, and have it abundantly," encapsulates the heart of the gospel: *God desires our flourishing.* This life is not a mere afterthought or a distant heavenly reward; it is a present, tangible reality that confronts oppressions and uplifts broken spirits. As we've journeyed through the teachings of Jesus, we've seen how each call—whether "Blessed are the poor in spirit" or "Love your enemies"—ultimately points us to a reality where justice and joy coexist.

For Black women, claiming abundant life requires both personal faith and communal effort. It involves unlearning scarcity mentalities and trusting that God's generosity extends even when the world's systems say otherwise. It also demands that we engage the world through the lens of liberation, ensuring that our freedom contributes to the liberation of others. In this way, we bear witness to the transformative power of Christ—a power that does more than save souls; it renews minds, redeems institutions, and breathes joy into every act of resistance and grace.

As you close this chapter, may you step boldly into the fullness Jesus promises. May every area of your life—spiritual, emotional, relational, and societal—reflect the boundless love and justice of the God who has called you by name. Rejoice in your identity as a beloved child of the Most High, destined for a life marked by resilience, communal care, and unshakeable hope. *This* is the abundant life that no thief can ever truly rob— one rooted in the unstoppable, liberating promise of Jesus Christ.

Continuing the Journey in Faith

Throughout this book, we have journeyed through ten of Jesus' most transformational teachings—each one resonating with *shameless audacity*, perseverance, communal support, and divine empowerment. From "Blessed Are the Poor in Spirit" to "I Have Come That They May Have Life . . . to the Full," we have seen how Jesus' words speak directly to the lived realities of Black women. They challenge us to embrace vulnerability, truth, humility, and hope in a world that often demands the opposite.

- **Shameless Audacity**: We are invited to approach God and life with bold persistence, daring to believe that our prayers and actions matter.

- **Perseverance in the Face of Injustice**: Systemic racism, sexism, and socio-economic barriers can feel insurmountable, but faith fortifies us to press forward, trusting in God's ultimate victory.

- **Communal Support and Solidarity**: None of us thrive in isolation. Jesus' example highlights the power of community—praying together, bearing one another's burdens, and building collective resilience.

- **Divine Empowerment**: Ultimately, our strength does not arise from sheer willpower but from the Holy Spirit's presence, guiding and sustaining us in every endeavor.

As you reflect on these lessons, allow them to shape your sense of identity and purpose. Remember that every principle we discussed—whether it's self-denial for the sake of Christ or seeking first God's kingdom—forms a holistic blueprint for living with hope, agency, and a deep commitment to justice.

Next Steps for the Reader

Faith is not static; it's a dynamic, evolving journey that invites continual growth. Below are a few suggestions to help you carry the insights from this book into your everyday life and community.

Recommended Readings
Womanist Theology

- *In Search of Our Mothers' Gardens* by Alice Walker (the term "womanist" originates from her work)
- *Sisters in the Wilderness: The Challenge of Womanist God-Talk* by Delores S. Williams
- *Just a Sister Away* by Renita J. Weems

Liberation Theology

- *A Theology of Liberation* by Gustavo Gutiérrez
- *Doing Christian Ethics from the Margins* by Miguel A. De La Torre
- *The Cross and the Lynching Tree* by James H. Cone

Intersectional Studies

- *Sister Outsider* by Audre Lorde (not strictly theological, but formative for intersectional thinking)
- *The Womanist Reader* edited by Layli Maparyan

Spiritual Practices and Community Projects
Spiritual Practices

- **Lectio Divina**: Meditatively read Scripture passages, focusing on how they speak to issues of justice and personal growth.
- **Journaling**: Document prayers, reflections, and small victories to see God's faithfulness over time.
- **Contemplative Retreats**: Schedule quiet retreats—solo or with a group—to replenish your spirit.

Community-Based Projects

- **Local Advocacy**: Volunteer with organizations addressing police reform, voter registration, or educational equity.
- **Church-Led Initiatives**: Encourage your congregation to host workshops on racial reconciliation, mental health, or economic empowerment.
- **Support Networks**: Form or join circles where women can share knowledge (e.g., financial literacy, entrepreneurship) and uplift each other's visions.

A Call to Ongoing Liberation Work

Discipleship is not a one-time commitment but a *lifelong* process. Jesus' message to the oppressed remains as urgent today as it was 2,000 years ago. He calls us to:

Stay Active in Pursuing Justice: Even when progress feels slow, continue advocating for fair policies, equitable resource distribution, and systemic transformation in your church, neighborhood, or broader society.

Nurture Wholeness and Wellness: Recognize that Jesus cares about both spiritual salvation and physical/emotional well-being. Seek professional counseling, healthy community relationships, and adequate rest.

Foster Bold Faith and Persistent Hope: Remember that each chapter highlighted Christ's call to maintain hope in God's power. Whether it's confronting personal hardships or societal ills, do not lose sight of God's faithfulness and ability to bring about lasting change.

As you carry forward the lessons of shameless audacity, poverty of spirit, loving enemies, and seeking the kingdom first, let them inform your daily choices. Every time you refuse to be silent in the face of injustice or step into a new leadership role, you embody the bold discipleship Jesus describes.

A Benediction for Bold Discipleship

Holy One,

You who see and care for the oppressed,

Bless each reader with unwavering courage and grace.

Let Your Spirit guide their steps,

Reminding them that in Christ, they are free to think big, pray boldly, and act justly.

Empower them to speak truth to power,

To embrace joy in the midst of trials,

And to share the abundance of Your kingdom with those most in need.

May their hearts remain tender yet strong,

Their spirits unbroken by adversity,

And their hope anchored in the promise of resurrection life.

As they continue this journey in faith,

Surround them with a community of fellow believers—

Sisters and brothers committed to love, liberation, and solidarity.

Grant them wisdom, creativity, and the holy audacity to believe

That the world can be reshaped by acts of justice and compassion.

In the name of Jesus, our Liberator and Friend,

Amen.

With this prayer, we acknowledge that the work of liberation is ongoing, yet we do not travel alone. God's power and presence accompany us—along with the rich inheritance of wisdom from those who have gone before us. May you step boldly into the next chapter of your faith, ever mindful of the Holy Spirit who energizes your calling, upholds your spirit, and secures your hope in a better tomorrow.

Go forth in confidence, Beloved— embracing the truth that God has indeed called you to live with SHAMELESS AUDACITY and unyielding faith!

About People of the Way Ministries

People of the Way Ministries is dedicated to making the transformative gospel of Jesus Christ—one of radical love, reconciliation, justice, and mercy—accessible to all. Rooted in the belief that God's presence is living and active in our daily lives, we create spiritual resources that can be engaged with on the go, meeting people wherever they are on their journey of faith.

Our ministry is built on four core principles:

1. **We love everyone.** We welcome and support all, especially those who have historically been excluded from full and loving fellowship in the body of Christ. We have dedicated ministries for LGBTQ communities, individuals in recovery, and those seeking justice and healing.

2. **We love God.** Through theological education, prayer, and intentional spiritual growth, we cultivate deeper relationships with the Divine.

3. **We embrace spiritual transformation.** We believe that through Christ's life, death, and resurrection, we are continually shaped into the people God has called us to be—inside and out.

4. **We spread the gospel in love and truth.** Through podcasts, blogs, online workshops, and faith-based discussions, we create spaces for reflection, challenge, and encouragement in the Christian walk.

To learn more about People of the Way Ministries, explore resources, and connect with our faith-based community, visit us online at **www.peopleoftheway.faith.**

Follow My Writing

If you have found encouragement and insight in these pages, I invite you to continue this journey with me. I regularly share reflections on faith, writing, and spiritual growth at **www.ngozirobinson.com**. There, you'll find all of my books, blog posts, upcoming projects, and ways to stay connected.

www.ingramcontent.com/pod-product-compliance
Lightning Source LLC
Chambersburg PA
CBHW060326050426

42449CB00011B/2666